T H
Hear

MW00528298

BOOKS BY DENG MING-DAO

THE WAY OF
Heart & Beauty

THE TAO OF DAILY LIFE

TRANSLATIONS FROM
THE THREE TEACHINGS,
SELECTED AND EDITED BY

Deng Ming-Dao

H
R
HAMPTON ROADS

Grateful acknowledgment to Professor Aimin Shen, Hanover
College, for her close reading.

Copyright © 2019 by Deng Ming-Dao

All rights reserved. No part of this publication may be reproduced or
transmitted in any form or by any means, electronic or mechanical, including
photocopying, recording, or by any information storage and retrieval system,
without permission in writing from Red Wheel/Weiser, LLC. Reviewers may
quote brief passages.

Cover design by Deng Ming-Dao

Cover photograph: *Woman's Sleeveless Jacket with Butterflies*. Late 19th–
early 20th century, China; Tapestry-woven silk and metallic thread (kesi);
27 x 36 in. (68.6 x 91.4 cm); Gift of Florance Waterbury, 1945;
The Metropolitan Museum of Art, New York.

Floral image by Qian Weicheng (1720–1772); album, ink on paper;
27.4 × 37 cm; National Palace Museum, Taipei, Taiwan.

Interior design by Deng Ming-Dao
Typeset at Side By Side Studios, San Francisco

Hampton Roads Publishing Company, Inc.
Charlottesville, VA 22906
Distributed by Red Wheel/Weiser, LLC
www.redwheelweiser.com

Sign up for our newsletter and special offers by going to
www.redwheelweiser.com/newsletter.

ISBN: 978-1-57174-839-3

Library of Congress Cataloging-in-Publication Data available upon request.

Printed in the United States of America
M&G

10 9 8 7 6 5 4 3 2 1

Contents

Introduction

We live in an era rich with more information than any previous period in the world's history. Each day, we consume an abundance of news, entertainment, and communication. We investigate other cultures, world views, theories, philosophies, and religions. When we're faced with serious questions, we rightly look into a vast stream of knowledge for answers, and soon we will find references to Taoism, Confucianism, and Buddhism.

Over thousands of years, these traditions have examined how to find our proper place in nature, make the right decisions, be moral leaders, face good and bad fortune, treat other living creatures, respect the earth, and view life and death calmly. The process began with those called the Early Kings. It continued with great philosophers such as Laozi, Zhuangzi, Confucius, and Buddha. They directed us toward a brilliant way that lasts to the present.

We certainly need the answers that path offers. We may be occupied with important issues and we may prize innovation, but we must still grapple with the same personal matters that have puzzled every generation and every people before us. War, starvation, inequality, corruption, human rights, emotions, relationships, family concerns, and mortality confront us all. The signposts that the ancients left unselfishly for us can point us to the best way.

The sages urge us to walk in the center of the road rather than to lurch side to side, to avoid being lost on detours, and to reject the manipulations of power-hungry autocrats. They urge us to embrace simplicity, compassion, honest livelihoods, and spirituality. It's all there for us to read for ourselves.

That raises three issues. First, the classics are unevenly translated. Some have been rendered repeatedly, while others are not well-known. This implies that some might be more "popular," but the fact is that they are more easily translated. Second, the language itself is old and poetic. Chinese words are ideographs and ancient grammar was not always linear, which leads to multiple interpretations. Each word therefore has many meanings that shift with the context. This detail delighted those writers who loved rhymes, wordplay, and expansive allusions. The language became incredibly concise and intense: occasionally, it takes two lines in English plus a glossary to reasonably translate a few words from the Chinese. Third, most of the classics have been previously translated with a dry and lofty tone—when they were just as often emotional records and incisive insights into the human condition.

In order to address that, this book looks at a number of classics, juxtaposing them so that they can comment on each other. This allows the reader to interpret them directly, and to benefit from the full range of viewpoints. The translation has been kept as spare as possible to retain the flavor of the originals.

The passages in this book pertain to two words: "heart" and "beauty." These two words are important precisely because they're challenging to translate. The Chinese word for "heart" means both "heart" and "mind" simultaneously, and the word for "beauty" describes a range of ideas from pleasurable sights to the highest excellence.

The ideograph for "heart" is a picture of a human heart: *xin*, 心. It means heart, mind, intention, center, core, intelligence, and soul all at once. The ideograph for beauty is *mei*, 美, meaning beautiful, satisfactory, good, or pleasing. It combines the sign for ram, 羊, over a glyph, 大, that means big, vast, great, large, or high. Perhaps we might picture a flock of sheep in a pastoral setting as the symbol of beauty. In earlier times, however, older forms of the word showed a feathered headdress on a person. Beauty was a shaman crowned with feathers—someone dancing with all their heart.

Translators usually choose "mind" for heart, and they often give some social or moral equivalent for "beauty." They ask a reader to remember the multiple meanings, but subliminally, it still matters if we're only reading "mind." To propose just rendering "heart" instead may be just as difficult, but reading heart and beauty gives the wisdom a greater impact: we see the feeling behind the lofty thoughts.

We often say, "My heart wants one thing, but my mind wants another." This use of the word heart was no different in my childhood. I heard my grandmother thank others for favors, kindnesses, or gifts by saying, "You have heart." If an aunt uttered something impolite, she quickly added, "I didn't have heart," which meant, "I didn't mean to hurt you." If an uncle complained about exhausting work, he said, "I have no heart for this." When my father recounted what he silently thought during an argument, he told us, "My heart said . . ." When my mother counseled me to look at the truth of a situation, she would ask, "What does your heart say?" When disappointment and loss struck the family, I heard elders whisper, "My heart aches." All this shows that we're neither referring to the mind as the thinking brain nor the heart as physical pump. We're referring to our total selves.

Any of us would say that the word "heart" includes our emotional nature. The word "mind" alludes to the intellect, rationality, and logic. The heart is tangible. It's beating in each of our chests right now. The mind is normally seen as intangible. We argue over whether it's really in the brain because we cannot show the mechanism of thought. (We can't show the mechanism of the heart's emotion and intuition either, in spite of pointing to valves and ventricles.) By seeing the heart in the chest and the brain in the head, we incorporate a fundamental split into our self-image. If you adopt the Chinese way, though, that division vanishes, and a new paradigm appears.

Our hearts love beauty. We might not each find the same things beautiful, but we each know the beauty that appeals to us. We decorate our houses; we are attracted to certain people; we long to go into nature; we listen to music; and we look at art, design, and fashion. When mathematicians and scientists talk about "elegant solutions," they're talking about beautiful ideas. We know what beauty is, and we go to it.

Beauty bridges that illusory rift between heart and mind. It encompasses emotion, intuition, thought, and analysis, and it inspires us. The recognition of beauty requires both heart and mind. If you accept the premise of this book, heart and mind are one.

Almost every selection for this book has the word "heart" or "beauty" in it. A surprising number have both. On a few occasions, supporting texts have been added to expand on the allusions in adjacent stories.

Our hearts love beauty; beauty opens our hearts.

THE THREE TEACHINGS

Most of the material in this book has been drawn from the Three Teachings: Confucianism, Buddhism, and Taoism. These are the major philosophical traditions of ancient China, and they are symbolized in this 1565 rubbing from the Shaolin Temple. A single person is made up of three people, representing Confucianism on the viewer's left, Buddhism in the center, and Taoism on the viewer's right. They hold one scroll, representing a united teaching.

The Chinese classics, and the overall culture at large, were shaped by these three traditions. The sixteenth-century novel, *Investiture of the Gods,* stated: "The Three Teachings are the gold and cinnabar of Taoism, the relics of Buddhist figures, as well as the Confucian virtues of humanity and righteousness. They are basically one tradition." On the other hand, they each have different emphases. Roughly speaking, Confucianism advocates ethics, morality, and a strong social hierarchy. Buddhism speaks of ethics, compassion, meditative stillness, and enlightenment. Taoism declares that the natural is the greatest good, that people should be free, and that "nonaction" (to live effortlessly) is best. These are approximations—after many centuries, scholars make many nuanced distinctions. Nevertheless, Chinese culture was so massive, and its standards were so toweringly high, that it needed all three teachings to maintain its balance. Only a combination of the Three Teachings could serve as a full and complete philosophy for a nation that was diverse, complicated, and millennia-old.

The passages presented here are drawn from the greatest philosophical texts of China. From Taoism, we have the *Daodejing* by the Taoist sage, Laozi; *Zhuangzi,* the eponymous book by that satirical and humorous philosopher; *Liezi,* filled with piercing stories; and *Wenzi,* a book that extended the thoughts of Laozi. Representing Confucianism is the *Analects,* which records quotations from Confucius; *Mengzi,* who is considered second only to Confucius; *Xunzi,* by the philosopher who believes in self-cultivation; and portions of the Confucian canon such as the *Book of Rites* and the *Classic of Poetry.* Buddhism provides a diverse set of sources, including the famous *Wumenguan,* the major collection of Zen gong'an (koans) and commentaries; the *Heart Sutra,* the *Platform Sutra,* and other scriptures; and poems from important figures such as Hanshan and Wang Wei. Finally, to round out the collection, there are other writings that also focus on heart and beauty. The passages are intermixed so that they can be compared, and to show how deep and widespread the consideration of heart and beauty has been.

Collecting the texts in this way is consistent with early writings. Most of them begin by quoting a famous master. For example, many texts begin: "The Master said . . ." or "Laozi said . . ." At first, that was a simple recording of a teaching. Later, people used that convention to expand on them. Wenzi is an example of that. But then, especially in the case of Zhuangzi and Liezi, they made Confucius, his students, powerful kings, and famous beauties into figures at the center of satirical and sometimes critical stories. Sometimes they dropped pretense altogether and used fictional characters or remade fables. In addition, each book is a jumble of legends, more like anthologies in their flavor. They were never created as logical and cumulative book-long arguments. Instead, they were presented as reality itself appeared: pure experience. To help with this, "Notes, Glossary, and Sources" at the end of this book gives explanation for those who are interested. Otherwise, the reader is left free to explore these teachings as directly as they were intended.

The source note at the end of each entry is followed by a letter distinguishing whether the text is Taoist Ⓣ, Confucian Ⓒ, or Buddhist Ⓑ. In a few cases, the entry is from the general literature of China, and is designated by Ⓛ.

Like the classics, this book isn't meant to be read all at once. Instead, read an entry at a time, or even just a paragraph at a time. Give it a chance to resonate. The thoughts are compressed. But every word is true, and you'll have more than enough to reward a slow approach.

THE WORD AT THE HEART OF IT ALL: TAO

Each one of the Three Teachings uses the word *Tao*, 道, as a central concept. The written word for Tao shows a person, in the form of a head: 首 (the "v" shape at the top represents two tufts of hair, the rectangle represents the face). That symbol is combined with the sign for stepping: 辶. (The sign was originally written as 辵, which is a symbol for feet.) Tao is a person walking. Since the head also represents a chief, it can also imply a person leading others on a path.

Over the centuries, this metaphor was loaded with many meanings: way, road, or path; direction; principle, truth, reason; to say, speak, talk, question, command; method, skill, and steps in a process. If that's bewildering, it can be summarized as this: Tao is the path of the entire cosmos. It is also the path of a person's life, which should be in harmony with the universal Tao. It is the method of being righteous and benevolent, of leading a simple life, and of seeking spiritual truth.

Every selection in this book is about finding the heart and beauty of Tao.

We live in a world metaphorically referred to as heaven and earth. Heaven is the divine power of all that initiates. It contains the sun and the moon, the weather, and the cycles of time by way of day and night and the seasons. Earth is the power that receives, grows, nurtures, and regenerates. Heaven drops a seed from the windy sky, waters it, and quickens it with the sun—but only if that seed is bedded in the earth. The seasons may occur as a result of heaven's turning, but it is the earth that brings forth all the myriad plants, trees, crops, and fruit.

Heaven and earth are seen as being impersonal. They are self-generating and self-perpetuating. No god is said to have created this world. No divine authority administers it. However, heaven and earth work in orderly ways: observing and contemplating them reveal the principles behind nature. It is upon these principles that human beings sought to base their philosophy.

The world of Tao seems to portray a feudal and agrarian one. Lest we think that irrelevant to our cities of gleaming highrises, soaring planes, and speeding cars, look how we still need leaders, how those leaders need to care for the populace, and how no amount of technology invalidates the need to feed people. Frankly, the texts seems surprisingly relevant: the passages warn against corrupt officials, those who would rely on military force, those who chase fame and wealth, and those who value ambition over community. The sages have to find a way to bring balance to the world in spite of these unfortunate people. Each thoughtful person has to find the right way to live. If one looks to the principles behind the stories, one finds immediate resonance.

Tao is a person on a path. Imagine that path to be one where we till our fields and go home at night content with our day's work. We are with our family, the cooking fires are warm, and the house is at peace. This is the life of heart and beauty. There is no better Way.

1 | The heart of a great person

A great person won't lose their infant heart.

Mengzi, "Li Lou II" ©

2 | Not going against Tao

Whoever really cherishes Tao
    is like a child.
Wasps, scorpions, and snakes won't bite,
    fierce beasts won't pounce,
    and raptors won't strike.
A child's bones and muscles are soft,
    but their grasp is firm.
Not yet knowing the union of male and female,
    all their organs are complete and their vigor is full.
Crying all day without becoming hoarse
    shows full harmony.
Knowing harmony is constancy.
Knowing constancy is clarity.
    But trying to improve upon life is a bad sign.

The heart uses the body's energy, and that's called strength.
Whatever grows strong grows old;
    we call that going against Tao.
Whatever goes against Tao
    comes to an early end.

Daodejing, 55 Ⓣ

1

3 | For the heart that won't do what's natural

Confucius reached the age of fifty-one, but he had still not fully learned of Tao. He went south to the land of Pei to see Lao Dan.

"You've come, haven't you?" Lao Dan asked. "I have heard that you are the most capable person in the north. Have you realized Tao?"

"Not yet."

"How have you sought it?"

"At first, I sought it through measures and numbers. After five years, I still hadn't realized it."

"Then how did you seek it again?"

"I then sought it through yin and yang, but still did not find it after twelve years."

"Of course. If Tao could be presented, then subjects would give Tao to their rulers. If Tao could be given, then people would give it to their parents. If Tao could be told to others, then all people would tell it to their siblings. If Tao could be bequeathed to others, then people would give it to their children and grandchildren.

"The reason for this is nothing other than:

"Inwardly, there is no one to direct it; and so it is unstoppable. Outwardly, it does not conform to our rules, and so it seems to us as if no one moves it. Tao emerges from the center and cannot be taken by what is outside. Similarly, the sage does not go out, does not enter into externals, and so the external cannot enter the center. The sage does not need to hide."

Fame is in the realm of the public. We shouldn't seek it much. Benevolence and righteousness are like the thatched huts of the ancients: we can stay in them overnight, but we can't dwell there for long. We can meet there, but we can't station ourselves there.

The realized people in the past used benevolence as they traveled the Tao. They used benevolence like someone staying in a hut overnight. That's how they wandered and roamed in emptiness, found sustenance in the fields of carefree simplicity, and stood in gardens without debt.

To ramble far, use nonaction. For carefree simplicity, look for easy nurturing. To be debt-free, don't spend. The ancients called this "wandering to collect the true."

Those who exist for wealth cannot give up their incomes. Those who exist for distinction cannot give up their fame. Those who crave power cannot delegate it to others. While they hold these things, they are unstable. As they live with them, they are melancholy. Yet they won't even look once in the mirror, or even consider resting for a moment. They are heaven's cursed people.

Hatred and kindness; taking and giving; admonishment and teaching; life and death. These are the eight standards. Can you comply with them and yet go through all the great changes of life without sinking? You have to be able to use them. The ancients say: "To rectify is to be correct."

For the heart that won't do what's natural, heaven's gate will never open.

Zhuangzi, "The Movement of Heaven" Ⓣ

4 | How long it takes to follow your heart

At fifteen, I set my will on learning.
At thirty, I was independent.
At forty, I had no doubts.
At fifty, I knew heaven's commands.
At sixty, my ears obeyed.
At seventy, I could follow what my heart desired
and not exceed the right measure.

Analects, "Wei Zheng" ©

5 | When Confucius reached the age of sixty

Zhuangzi said to Huizi: "When Confucius reached the age of sixty, he changed. What he first believed to be right he suddenly rejected as wrong. He hadn't realized that what he thought was true for fifty-nine years was no longer valid."

Huizi said: "Confucius was earnest in pursuing the acquisition of knowledge."

"Confucius rejected such a course; he never claimed to be doing such a thing. This is what he said: 'People get their talents from the great root. They should return to the spiritual in this life.' Their singing should be in tune with pitch pipes. Their speech should be as suitable as the law. When gain and righteousness are set before them, others should remark on how they weigh good and bad, true and false, straight and bent. In order to make people use their hearts, they urge cooperation rather than obstinance. Ahh! I have not caught up to him!"

Zhuangzi, "Fables" ⊤

6 | Human nature is good

When it comes to human nature, it is basically good.
That is what is meant by excellence.
If people act badly, it isn't a matter of their potential.

All people have compassion in their hearts.
All people have reservation and shame in their hearts.
All people have reverence and respect in their hearts.
All people have a sense of right and wrong in their hearts.

Compassion in their hearts
     leads to kindness.
Reservation and shame in their hearts
     leads to righteousness.
Reverence and respect in their hearts
     leads to the proper.
Right and wrong in their hearts
     leads to knowledge.

Kindness, righteousness, propriety, and knowledge
don't fuse into me from the outside.
They are part of my own strength.
If you don't think of those aspects,
you don't want to be aware of them.

Therefore:
     Seek and you will find them.
     Ignore them and you will lose them.

Mengzi, "Gaozi I" ©

7 | When nothing is hidden

Liezi went to study with a teacher.

After the third year, his heart did not dare think of right and wrong. His mouth did not dare to speak of gain and loss. But his teacher, Lao Shang, barely glanced at him.

After the fifth year, his heart thought less of right and wrong. His mouth spoke less of gain and loss. His teacher's face relaxed and he smiled.

After the seventh year, the thoughts in his heart were submissive, and he barely considered right and wrong. His mouth was compliant, and he seldom spoke of gain and loss. His teacher invited him to bring a mat and sit beside him.

After the ninth year, the thoughts in his heart were placid. The words from his mouth were serene. Significantly, he did not consider right and wrong or gain and loss for himself— nor did he consider right and wrong or gain and loss for others. Outer and inner merged.

After that, his eyes were like ears. His ears were like his nose. His nose was like his mouth. His mouth had nothing to which it could be compared. His heart was still, his body was relaxed, his bones and flesh were in complete harmony. He was not conscious of needing a body. His feet left no tracks. His heart had few thoughts. He seemed to hoard his words.

Finally, he went on his way because nothing was hidden from him.

Liezi, "Confucius" ⊤

8 | What sages ponder

Laozi said: When the leaders of people ponder, their spirits do not race through their chests, their knowledge doesn't go beyond the four quarters, and they keep benevolence and sincerity in their hearts.

The sweet rain falls with timeliness. The Five Crops grow luxuriantly. Spring sprouts, summer ripens. Autumn brings harvests, winter is the time to store. Reviews are made monthly, reports are given seasonally, and tithes are given yearly.

The leaders nurture all people equitably. They inspire awe by being sincere, honest, and true. Their methods are minimal and confuse no one, and they civilize people impressively. Their laws are lenient, they are slow to mete out punishment, and their prisons stand empty. The world follows a single standard without any defilements of the heart.

This is what sages ponder.

Wenzi, "Sincerity" Ⓣ

9 | Work as a compassionate person

The heart is like a great and boundless ocean
plant pure lotuses widely to cultivate body and heart.
Keep both your hands free of worldly involvements,
and work as a compassionate person in this world.

Blue Cliff Record Ⓑ

10 | Truly study

Truly study Buddha: don't be attached to body, heart, or
worldly affairs.

This is great generosity.

Truly study Buddha: don't generate greed, hatred, or
ignorance.

This is great morality.

Truly study Buddha: don't calculate the rights and wrongs
of others or oneself.

This is great tolerance.

Truly study Buddha: don't be disruptive or distracted.

This is great diligence.

Truly study Buddha: don't keep deluded thoughts or
pursue them.

This is great concentration.

Truly study Buddha: don't be confused by delusion.

This is great wisdom.

Ouyi Zhixu (1599–1655), "Song of the Six Perfections in Studying Buddha" Ⓑ

11 | Free your heart, but don't lose it

Kindness is your heart.

Righteousness is your road.

Keep to your road; do not lose it.

Free your heart and don't look elsewhere.

That would be sad!

If you lose your chickens or dogs,
you know to look for them.
But too many who lose their hearts,
don't think to look for them!

The Tao of learning and inquiry is nothing more
than to look for your own lost heart.

Mengzi, "Gaozi I" ©

12 | A good heart comes with depth

The greatest good is to be like water.
The good of water is that it benefits
all things without conflict.
It flows in places that people despise,
and so, it's akin to Tao.

A good dwelling comes from the earth,
a good heart comes with depth,
a good ally comes from kindness,
a good word comes from trust,
a good government comes from rule,
a good outcome comes from ability,
a good movement comes from timing.

One who has such goodness does not fight
and is therefore free of fault.

Daodejing, 8 ⓣ

THE
WAY
OF
H
E
A
R
T
&
B
E
A
U
T
Y

13 | Protect your true heart

My heart is like the autumn moon.
The azure lake is pure, bright, and clear.
Since nothing can compare,
tell me, how could I speak?

Anger is a fire in the heart;
it can burn down a forest of virtue.
To practice the Tao of bodhisattvas,
endure humiliation, protect your true heart.

Hanshan (Tang Dynasty), *Selected Poems of Hanshanzi* Ⓑ

14 | Live in your heart

If your heart has been exhausted
you will know your character.
If you know your character
you will know heaven.

Live in your heart,
nourish your nature,
and serve heaven.

If you don't think twice
about dying too soon
or growing too old,

but you cultivate yourself
with patience instead, you will be
    set for life.

Mengzi, "Jin Xin I" ©

15 | The sages ruled by opening hearts

Not singling some out as better
    will keep people from fighting.
Not prizing goods as costly and rare
    will keep people from stealing.
Not showing what stokes desire
    will keep hearts from tangling.

The sages ruled by opening hearts,
filling bellies, soothing wills,
and strengthening bones.
They always kept the people
free of thought or desires—
    for where there was thought
    the cunning were sure to act on it.
    Where there were no such deeds,
    all was peaceful.

Daodejing, 3 ⓣ

11

16 | Keeping the natural beauty of the heart

The trees of Bull Mountain were once beautiful. But they were on the edge of a great country and men used axes to chop them down. How was there beauty anymore?

Still, through steady growth for day and night, and watering by rain and dew, buds and sprouts returned. That drew cattle and goats to graze. The slopes were again stripped bare. People who saw the bald peak never thought timber had been there. But we couldn't call that the mountain's true nature.

In the same way, should we say that there is no natural kindness or justice in your heart? If you lose your good heart, like a mountain that has had all its trees gradually chopped down, how will your heart keep its beauty?

It's not likely that beauty will grow back over time. You won't be able to distinguish the good and bad of others, even if you sit in the calm breath of dawn. You will be fettered or destroyed by the next day. This oppression will go on and no amount of effort on your part will bring any quick relief. When all has been ruined, your heart won't be any different from that of a wild bird or animal.

When we happen to see savage people, we might not imagine that they ever had any potential for good. But how can that be the right view of human nature?

Anything will grow and thrive if it receives the right nourishment. Deny that nourishment, and everything declines and falls away. Confucius said: "Hold it and it stays with you. Let it go and you lose it."

He was talking about your heart!

Mengzi, "Gaozi I" ©

17 | Use your heart as a mirror

Don't try to control fame. Don't try to be a storehouse of future plans. Don't try for career and office. Don't try to be the lord of all wisdom.

Embody everything to the fullest and leave no trace wherever you go. Fulfill all that you have received from heaven, but don't see yourself as getting anything. Be empty, and let that be all.

The perfect person uses their heart as a mirror. It conveys nothing, it receives nothing. It responds, but does not take. Such a person can triumph over anything without risking hurt.

Zhuangzi, "The Normal Course for Emperors and Kings" Ⓣ

18 | Cleave to beauty

Youzi said: "In putting propriety to use, prize harmony. The Tao of the Early Kings was to cleave to beauty. Great and small follow it."

Analects, "Xue Er" Ⓒ

19 | How to be great

The disciple Gong Du asked: "Everyone is equal. Yet some people are great and some people are petty. Why is that?"

"Those who follow their own greatness become great," Mengzi replied. "Those who follow their own pettiness remain small."

"Everyone is equal. But some follow their greatness while others follow their pettiness. How can that be?"

"Our senses, such as hearing and seeing, provide information, but they cannot think. They cover only external things, following from one to another as they gather them in. The heart is a place of consciousness, and thinking there brings understanding. If we don't think, we don't comprehend."

Heaven gave everything to us. If we make it our priority to stay with what is great, then pettiness will have no place. This is what makes a great person.

Mengzi, "Gaozi I" ©

20 | Autumn Floods

The season for autumn floods arrived. Hundreds of streams poured into the river and the currents swelled drastically. The distance from one shore to the other grew so wide that one could distinguish neither cattle nor horses. The river god, He Bo (Earl of the River), was overjoyed because he thought that he now possessed all the world's beauty.

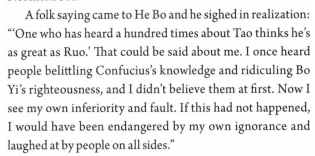

He Bo strode eastward along the river's course until he came to the Northern Sea. He stood looking further to the east and could see no end to the waters. As he slowly turned his face over the endless waves, he saw Ruo, the God of the Northern Sea.

A folk saying came to He Bo and he sighed in realization: "'One who has heard a hundred times about Tao thinks he's as great as Ruo.' That could be said about me. I once heard people belittling Confucius's knowledge and ridiculing Bo Yi's righteousness, and I didn't believe them at first. Now I see my own inferiority and fault. If this had not happened, I would have been endangered by my own ignorance and laughed at by people on all sides."

Ruo of the Northern Sea said, "You can't discuss the ocean with a frog in a well; it thinks its narrow confines are an enormous space. You can't talk to a summer insect about ice; it only knows its one season. You can't discuss Tao with a scholar; they are trapped in their teachings. Now, you have come from your riverbed and you have seen the great ocean. You have confronted your own inadequacy. So take all that you're about to hear as a great philosophy:

"Of all the waters under heaven, none are so great as the ocean. Ten thousand rivers return to it, and we will never know a time when they will be filled. In turn, the oceans keep draining, and we will never know a time when they will be emptied. Whether spring or autumn, these facts don't change, and it doesn't matter whether there are floods or drought. The oceans are supreme over rivers such as the flowing Yangzi or Yellow Rivers, and they cannot be measured or counted.

"Nevertheless, I have not made much of myself. I have never compared myself to heaven or earth, or the energy I receive from yin and yang. I live between heaven and earth, no different than a pebble or a sapling set upon an enormous mountain. Since I realize that I am so tiny, why should I make so much of myself?

"Consider that all the four seas between heaven and earth may not be much more than what a pile of stones are to a huge marsh. Consider that our entire nation compared to the size of an ocean is smaller than a grain of rice in a huge granary. Out of all the things in this world that number in the millions, human beings are only one of them. Although people occupy all nine states, if you compare them to all the creatures who live by eating, or the far distances that boats and carriages travel, people are only one kind of creature. When put beside all the beings in the world, humanity is but one hair on the body of a horse.

"Now this includes the lineage of the Five Sovereigns, the struggles of the Three Emperors, the sorrow of honorable people, and the labors of all trustworthy persons in government. Bo Yi was famous for declining to serve his liege any longer. Confucius is praised for having had a wide impact. But both of them were making too much of themselves—just as, not long ago, you made much of yourself and your water."

"So should I consider heaven and earth as the greatest, and the tip of a hair as the smallest?"

"Not necessarily. Of people and things, there is no ultimate measure, and no exhaustion. Time never stops. Diversity never stops multiplying. Endings and beginnings are ongoing. That's why those of great wisdom see both distant and near, they do not see the small as insignificant nor the large as being stupendous, and they know that measurements differ endlessly. They examine the causes of events both ancient and modern without being troubled by how remote the past might be and they gather everything about the present effortlessly, for they know that time never stops. They examine filling and emptying, are not overjoyed by gain, and are not dismayed by loss, for they know that all must separate and nothing is permanent. They comprehend the level and quiet, and therefore they aren't giddy over life nor are they gloomy over death, for they know that endings and beginnings cannot be controlled. We must plan for what people know rather than what they do not know, for the time during their lives rather than for whatever time was there before they were born. When it comes to the small, or trying to fill what's enormous, people are confused and can find no outcome for themselves. In view of all this: How can you know that a hair is enough to express what is tiniest? How can you know that heaven and earth are enough to really define what is the largest?"

He Bo asked: "What is so valuable about Tao?"

Ruo of the Northern Sea replied: "To know Tao is to arrive at principle. To arrive at principle is to understand the power of authority. One who understands the power of authority won't allow anything to injure oneself.

"One who has realized virtue cannot be burned by fire or drowned by water. Neither cold nor heat can bring harm. Neither raptor nor beast can bring hurt. This doesn't mean that a person is unaware. It means that they distinguish safety and risk. One is serene whether in disaster or happiness and prudent whether going or coming and so nothing is harmful.

"Thus, it is said: heaven is a matter of the inner. People are a matter of the outer. Virtue is of this inner heaven. If you are a person who knows heaven as you move, then your root is heaven, and you have the right position in life. You will bend and stretch as you move at the right pace. You will have returned to what's necessary, and you will have found the utmost."

"What do you call heaven? What do you call people?"

"Cattle and horses have four legs: this was set by heaven. But when the heads of horses are bridled, and the noses of cattle are pierced, this is set by people. That's why it's said: 'Don't let the human wipe out what is set by heaven. Don't let your own plans wipe out what heaven ordains. Don't try to possess and die for fame.' Carefully guard this all and never lose it. That is called returning to the genuine."

Zhuangzi, "Autumn Floods" Ⓣ

21 | What is, is-not

Whether this heart or this Buddha, what-is,
>   is-not.
What is not-the-Buddha is not-the-heart, and what-is-not,
>   is-not.
Try to serve what-is and what-is-not as you sit in meditation.
Don't be concerned with what the heart and the Buddha
>   both rely upon.

Emperor Yongzheng (1678–1735), *Fo Guang Jiaokeshu* Ⓑ

22 | Why beauty matters to hearts in grief

Mengzi left Qi and went to Lu to bury his mother. When he returned to Qi, he stopped at Ying where Chong Yu said: "When you were here before, you asked me to supervise the making of her coffin, even if you didn't know if I was up to it. Under those circumstances, I didn't want to ask, but now I'll humbly ask you: was the wood we used too beautiful?"

Mengzi said, "Long ago, there were no rules about the inner and outer coffin. In time, both the inner and outer coffins were supposed to be seven inches thick for an emperor or a commoner alike. This is done not simply for the sake of a beautiful appearance but because it fully expresses all that is in the human heart.

"If we don't do this, no one will feel satisfied. The old people set this standard as long as they could afford it. Why should I not do the same? Death has transformed our kin. We don't want the earth to touch their skin, and that comforts our hearts.

"I have heard that a noble one will not shortchange their parents for anything in the world."

Mengzi, "Gong Sun Chou II" ©

23 | Help everyone get their own strength

Laozi said: A kind father who loves his child asks nothing in return. He will not divide his heart about this.

A sage nurtures the people because it's in their nature; they do not use others as officials do. Officials emphasize their own power and meritorious deeds, but it leads to exhaustion and does not perpetuate kindness.

Therefore, in order to have everyone's love, help everyone find their own strength. Raise everyone's happiness. Put contentment in everyone's hearts. If you see to that from the beginning, you will already know the outcome.

Wenzi, "Abstruse Understanding" ⊤

24 | Let people have steady hearts

Duke Wen of Teng asked Mengzi about the proper way to govern a country.

Mengzi replied, "None of the business for the people can be put off. The *Classic of Poetry* says:

> In the daylight, you gather grass,
> at night you braid your ropes.
> Then you must go quickly into your house
> for soon we must start sowing grain.

"The Tao of the people is this: if they can be productive on a regular basis, they will have steady hearts. If they cannot be productive all the time, their hearts will be unsteady.

"If their hearts are unsteady, they'll ignore the laws and do wrong freely. This is unavoidable. When they have been forced into crime like that, to pursue them and punish them is to trap them. What kind ruler would trap citizens?

"Therefore, a virtuous ruler must be respectful, temperate, and courteous to all under them. Whatever they take from the people must be limited.

"Yang Hu said: 'Pursue only wealth and you will not be benevolent. Pursue benevolence and you will not be rich.'"

Mengzi, "Teng Wen Gong I" ©

25 | Take the world as one nation

Laozi said: The son of heaven and the nobles should take the world as one nation and as one family and care for all living things as if they were their own farm animals.

But some regard the world as a vastness filled with an abundance of living creatures and they become charged with ambition and arrogance. The larger states invade the smaller ones by military force, and the smaller states haughtily mistreat their own subjects. Those who use the heart for the sake of extravagance and expansionism are like the whirlwind or rainstorm: they cannot last long.

Thus, the sage uses Tao to subdue such impulses, and to maintain unity and nonaction without damaging the surging energy of the times. They watch over the common people and observe softness. They are reserved and do not try to possess anything for themselves.

Their law emulates the rivers and seas. The rivers and seas are models of nonaction that achieve through the actions inherent in themselves rather than by means of power. They succeed best by flowing down the valleys of the world.

Hence, for the spirit not to die, one must love oneself. For there to be success, you must be worthy enough to fulfill ten thousand situations and to help ten thousand creatures achieve their own glory. Authority and office are of the utmost seriousness and should never be taken lightly. If you do, you will never achieve any merit or success.

In Tao, the small becomes the big, the many relies on the few. Therefore, the sage uses Tao to cope with the evils of the world. They are soft and delicate, subtle, and see to the small. They are frugal, sparing, decreasing, lessening, and see to the lacking. Those who see the small can then accomplish the large. Those who see the lacking can then accomplish the beautiful.

Wenzi, "Nine Guardings" ⓣ

26 | Crossing the Lingding Channel

Enduring hardship and struggle from the start,
poorly armed through four years of war,
pieces of my mountains and rivers scattered to the wind.
I'm left to sink and bob like rain-beaten duckweed.
Fearful Shoals was indeed terrifying;
crossing the Lonely Sea brought forlorn sighs.
Since ancient times, what person has never died?
Let me leave my red heart, shining in history.

Wen Tianxiang (1236–1283), "Crossing the Lingding Sea" ⓛ

27 | Paradise

Holy people dwell on Pike Mountain, surrounded by rivers and seas. They live by breathing the breezes and drinking dew, and they never eat the Five Grains. Their hearts are as deep as springs, their bodies have womanly gentleness. They are not sensual, and do not have the entanglements of love. They are led by immortals and sages.

No one is worried or angry. All are sincere and honest. They need no one's support, nor do they ask any favors, and yet they always had enough. No one covets or hoards, and yet no one ever lacks for anything.

Yin and yang always move. The sun and moon are always bright. The four seasons always remain in order. Wind and rain always come in constant proportions. They are always educated and literate. Each year's crop is always abundant.

And yet: The earth is never exhausted. People don't die prematurely and they don't get sick. No creature is diseased or suffers. The ghosts make no supernatural sounds.

Liezi, "The Yellow Emperor." ⊤

24

28 | The power of accumulation

If you accumulate enough dirt to make a mountain, wind and rain will come. If you accumulate enough water to make a gulf, then dragons will come to live in it. If you accumulate enough goodness to become virtuous, then you will naturally attain spiritual brilliance and perfect a sagely heart.

Therefore, without accumulating small steps, you cannot go a thousand miles. Without combining rivers, you cannot have the sea. A thoroughbred's leap cannot exceed ten strides, but a weak nag pulling a cart for ten days will accomplish more.

If you start to carve and give up, you won't even be able to break rotten wood. But if you carve without giving up, you'll be able to carve even metal and stone.

Xunzi, "Exhortation to Learning" ©

29 | The heart-way through no-gate

Buddhism takes the heart as its basis,
and no-gate as its gate to enlightenment.

If there is no-gate, then how will you go through?
What doesn't find the Tao to enter this gate
never finds their precious home.

What depends on circumstances
perishes from start to finish.

However, to speak this way
is to raise waves where there is no wind,
or to single out a sore on unblemished skin.
It dully seeks distinctions and order in words and verses.

If you swing sticks trying to hit the moon,
or scratch a shoe when your foot itches,
what chance will you have to enter?

Wumenguan, Preface Ⓑ

30 | The door to nothingness

Laozi said: Why do people of Tao travel? To reach emptiness.
What is at the heart of their journey? Supreme nothingness.
Spreading out in all directions, they walk to the gate of nothingness (wumen). They listen to the silence. They see the

formless. Then they are no longer confined to the times and they are no longer tied to custom.

This is why the sages move through the world. The True Person, however, or the great persons may try to rectify the world, but the sages don't advise them.

Ordinary people are constrained to the world. They seem stable and tied down, but their spirits drain away, and they are thus not spared the trouble of separation. If I am tied down, then my life will always be controlled by what is outside myself.

Wenzi, "Sincerity" ℗

31 | Like a binding around the heart

A worm does not benefit from claws or teeth, nor does it have powerful muscle and bone. It eats from the soil above it, and drinks from the Yellow Springs below it. It operates single-heartedly.

A crab has eight legs and two pincers, but if it were not for the holes left by snakes and eels, it would have no place to live. It operates with a frantic heart.

Therefore, it is said: if you don't first have a somber will, you won't reach the most luminous understanding. If you don't first feel confused about your work, you won't have radiant accomplishments. Try to go two ways at an intersection and you won't get anywhere. Work for two lords and it won't be seemly. Eyes cannot focus on two sights and still

27

be clear. Ears cannot listen for two sounds and still comprehend. A wingless dragon lacks legs but can fly, whereas a tree
rat has five kinds of genius and is still desperate. The *Classic
of Poetry* states:

> The cuckoo in the mulberry tree
> has seven offspring.
> The virtuous ones and the noble ones
> have a single righteousness.
> That single righteousness
> is like a binding around their hearts.

Xunzi, "Exhortation to Learning" Ⓒ

32 | The heart is like …

The heart goes like the wind;
    it cannot be grasped.
The heart flows like water;
    it appears and ceases, and is nonabiding.
The heart glows like fire;
    kindled from many causes.
The heart is like emptiness;
    defilements are impermanent.

Yijing (635–713), *Heap of Jewels Sutra* Ⓑ

33 | It's best is to effect spiritual change

Laozi said: If laws and rewards are established and yet customs still don't change, it's because our hearts lack sincerity. Therefore, listen to the people talk and you'll know their manners. Observe what brings them joy and you'll know what's popular. Examine their conventions and you'll know how to change them.

When people embrace truth and follow sincerity, it moves heaven and earth. Even the spirits will go beyond all bounds to comply. When sincerity pervades the Tao, the right intentions will be evident to all the people in the world without uttering a word. Even birds and beasts and the supernatural creatures will be transformed.

Therefore, it's best is to effect spiritual change. The next best is to make it impossible to do wrong. The lowest is to bestow rewards on the worthy and to punish the violent.

Wenzi, "Sincerity" Ⓣ

34 | My heart is not a stone

My heart is not a stone;
    yet it cannot be moved.
My mind is not a mat;
    yet it can't be rolled up.
Graceful and elegant,
    I cannot be reproached.

Classic of Poetry, "Bo Zhou" Ⓒ

35 | What moves?

A monastery banner flapped in the wind above the Sixth Patriarch (Huineng; 638–713). Two monks began to argue.

"It's the banner that moves," the first one said.

"It's the wind that moves," the other countered.

They argued back and forth without reaching any conclusion.

The Sixth Patriarch said: "It is not the wind that moves. It is not the banner that moves. Actually, it's your heart that moves."

The two monks were bewildered.

WUMEN (NO-GATE) SAID: "It is not the wind that moves. It is not the banner that moves. It is not the heart that moves. Where then do you see the patriarch? If you look into this closely and carefully, you will see that the two monks got gold when they were buying iron. The patriarch was unable to restrain his laughter and straightaway divulged it all.

WUMEN'S VERSE:
Wind, banner, heart, movement.
Instant blame and error.
Knowing only how to open one's mouth
with speech unconscious of fault.

Wumenguan, Case 29 Ⓑ

36 | The Tao of heaven and earth

Those who are lofty but without ingrained ideas,
cultivate themselves without needing ideas of benevolence
        or righteousness,
govern without claiming merit or fame,
are tranquil without the turbulence of rivers and seas,
are long-lived without artificial ways,
forget everything,
possess all,
and are of unlimited tranquility even as people follow in
        beauty.

That is the Tao of heaven and earth.
That is the virtue of the sages.

Zhuangzi, "Ingrained Ideas" ⑦

37 | Could he see with his ears and hear with his eyes?

When a man from Chen went to the state of Lu on business,
he visited his uncle and his uncle's family. The uncle said, "A
sage lives in my country."

"Do you mean Confucius?"

"Yes."

"How can you tell he's a sage?"

"I've always heard his student, Yan Hui, say: 'Confucius
can stop his heart but still use his body.'"

The man from Chen said: "My country also has sage. Did you not know that?"

"Who is that?"

"He's a student of Lao Dan named Kangcangzi (Master of the High Granary). He has gotten all of Lao Dan's Tao. His ears can see and his eyes can listen."

The Marquis of Lu was startled to hear of this. He ordered his ministers to send presents and an invitation to Kangcangzi.

When he arrived, the Marquis of Lu asked him humbly about what he had heard.

"That's mere rumor," said Kangcangzi. "I cannot change how ears and eyes are used, but I can see without using my eyes and hear without using my ears."

"That's even more extraordinary! What Tao can that be? This royal person would like to hear of that."

"My body is one with my heart. My heart is one with my breath. My breath is one with my spirit. My spirit is one with nothingness. Therefore I can naturally see what's there or detect any sound, whether it's farther than eight deserts or as close as inside my eyebrows and eyelashes. If it comes to me, I will surely know it. I don't distinguish whether I know through my seven openings, four limbs; my heart, belly, or six viscera; it's just that I know."

The Marquis of Lu was highly delighted, and on a later day, told this all to Confucius. Confucius laughed, but said nothing.

Liezi, "Confucius" Ⓣ

38 | Proper learning

What the noble one learns enters the ears and manifests in the heart, spreads through the four limbs, and stays in the body whether it's moving or still. Their slightest word and most subtle movements are immediate examples to others.

But what an inferior person learns enters the ears and exits the mouth. The distance from mouth to ears is but four inches. How could that be enough to bring beauty to a seven-foot body?

The ancients learned for their own sakes. Nowadays, students learn wanting to control others. When a noble one learns, they become beautiful. When an inferior person learns, they only want a means to an end. Thus, to speak without being asked is called arrogance. To give two answers to one question is called bombast. Arrogance is wrong. Bombast is wrong.

A noble one responds immediately like a struck bell.

Xunzi, "Exhortation to Learning" ©

39 | Base yourself in heaven's command

Laozi said: Base yourself on heaven's command; rule through a skilled heart; reason through like and dislike; follow through a natural disposition. All in all, find your rule though the pervasive Tao.

"Base yourself in heaven's command" means to experience disaster and happiness without doubt.

"Rule through a skilled heart" means not to be rash in happiness or anger.

"Reason through like and dislike" means not to be greedy and worthless.

"Follow through a natural disposition" means to counter desires with integrity.

"To experience disaster and happiness without doubt" means to have stillness-in-movement when conforming to circumstance.

To reason and "not to be rash in happiness or anger" means to negate reward and punishment.

"Not to be greedy and worthless" means not to harm one's inner nature with desire.

"To counter desires with integrity" means to maintain good health and to be content.

Make these four levels common throughout your life and seek nothing else. You won't have to make pretenses with anyone. You'll return to your true self.

Wenzi, "Nine Guardings" ⊤

40 | Zhaozhou's Dog

A monk asked Zhaozhou Congshen (778–897): does a dog have Buddha nature or no?

Zhaozhou answered: "No!"

WUMEN SAID: "To practice meditation, you must go through the mountain pass of the patriarchs. To attain subtle realization, you must exhaust your heart-road-thought until it vanishes.

If you don't go through the patriarch's mountain pass and your heart-road-thought does not vanish, then you will be like a spirit grabbing at brush and trees.

What Tao is the mountain pass of the patriarchs? It is this single word, "No." That is the patriarch's gate and the one mountain pass. That is why it is called Chan Buddhism's "No-gate-mountain-pass."

Once you go through and cross, you'll not only see Zhaozhou face-to-face, but you'll also go hand-in-hand with the succession of patriarchs, tangling your eyebrows with theirs, seeing and hearing the same as them.

Wouldn't that be quite gratifying?

Wouldn't you like to go through that mountain pass?

Wumenguan, Case 1 Ⓑ

41 | "I went today and arrived yesterday"

If each person took an integrated heart as their advisor, who would be without a teacher? Whether knowledgeable and logical or uneducated and foolish, no one would be stranded without guidance.

Yet if we have incomplete hearts, we are error-prone. We'll be like someone who says, "I went to Yue today and arrived yesterday." We'll take what is unreal as real. To take the unreal for the real—why, even the supernatural Yu the Great could not comprehend that, so how could I?

Words are not just foul blowing. Words have meaning. But if speech is uncertain, how will it make sense? How can speakers really know true speech? They think that their words are extraordinary, when they sound more like chirping chicks. What eloquence or reason could they have?

How can Tao be so secret that we should speak of true and false? How can speech be so obscure that we should speak of right and wrong? Where can we go where the Tao is not found? What can we eliminate as impossible?

Tao is obscured by small comprehension. Speech is obscured by glorious and flowery words. For example, we have the arguments between the Confucians and the Mohists. One side says yes, while the other says no; one side says no, while the other side says yes. Wanting to state what *is* means something else *is-not*; wanting to state *what-is-not* means something *is*. Only avoiding this leads to enlightenment.

Zhuangzi, "The Adjustment of Controversies" Ⓣ

42 | One who desires good

The person who desires good may be called excellent.
One who is completely thus may be called true.
One who is fully true may be called beautiful.
One who is fully true has a bright luster and so may be called
     great.
One who is great and can transform others may be called a
     sage.
One who is a sage, even if unknown to others, will be
     spiritual.

Mengzi, "Jin Xin II" ©

43 | The joy of heaven

Zhuangzi said: "My master! My master! My master blends
ten thousand things without committing any wrong, brings
vitality to ten thousand generations without needing benevolence, is older than the earliest antiquity and yet is not aged,
covers heaven and supports the earth, carves and shapes the
form of all people without ruining them. All that is called
Heavenly Joy.

"Consequently, it has been said that those who know
heaven's joy move like heaven throughout their lives. They
transform upon death as all other beings do, are still but with
a virtue that is the same as yin, and they move with a pulsa-
tion the same as yang. One who knows Heavenly Joy never

resents heaven, never condemns men, never bothers other creatures, and never blames ghosts.

"Accordingly, their movements are those of heaven, their stillness if that of earth. With one settled heart, they can rule the world. Ghosts cause them no trouble. The souls do not belabor him. With one settled heart, they care for the ten thousand things.

"Their words are open and serene, and yet resound throughout heaven and earth, and reach the ten thousand things. This is Heavenly Joy.

"Heavenly Joy is the heart of the sage who gathers all under heaven together."

Zhuangzi, "The Tao of Heaven" Ⓣ

44 | In the heart of heaven

A noble one's interchanges should be neutral as water.
Try to hold appearances and what seems close will be a
        thousand miles away.

Ask me whether this suits me
and I'm speechless before such future boundlessness.

Flowery branches, the full spring:
in the heart of heaven, the round moon.

Hongyi (1880–1942), *Complete Works of Master Hongyi* Ⓑ

45 | Beautiful learning

The noble one knows that learning that is not intact and not pure is insufficient to be beautiful. So they review by repeating and counting, ponder thoroughly, settle it in their very being, and eliminate anything harmful in order to sustain and nourish beauty.

If the eyes have no desire to look at what isn't right, if the ears have no desire to hear what isn't right, if the mouth have no desire to speak of what isn't right, and if the heart have no desire to worry about what isn't right, then one reaches the level of excellence.

Then the eyes are excellent in the five colors. The ears are excellent in the five tones. The mouth is excellent in the five flavors. The heart has the benefit of all under heaven.

As a result, neither power nor gain will disturb the noble one. The crowd will not shift them and nothing in the world will shake them. They live by this. They die by this. This is called holding virtue.

Holding virtue leads to being fixed. Being fixed leads to doing-as-one-should. Being fixed and doing-as-one-should is called being a complete person. Heaven will see their brilliance. Earth will see their light. The noble one values completeness.

Xunzi, "Exhortation to Learning" ©

I have hundreds of bones. Nine openings. Six viscera. My body is complete in these. Which part should I love the most?

Are you pleased with all your own parts equally? Or do you favor some over others? You have them all, and they serve you as faithfully as if they were assistants or servants. Yet despite being assistants or servants, none of them are capable of controlling all the others. Even all of them together could not do so. It seems that there must be a real controller among them, whether we can discover its true nature or not, or whether we can better know the truth of it or not.

Once we have our complete form, our parts continue to function until our end. It doesn't matter if they are sharply opposed or are divided against outside things, they rush on swiftly and cannot be stopped. Should that be called sad?

If we labor and labor to the end of our lives without achieving fulfillment, or if we are tired and exhausted from our work without knowing where it all goes—that might not be sorrowful and bad!

People won't speak of death, but what good is that? When the body undergoes death's change, the heart must go with it. Should that not be called a great sorrow?

Is the substance of a person's life that ephemeral? Am I the only one who sees that clue? Other people don't seem to see it!

Zhuangzi, "The Adjustment of Controversies" ⓣ

47 | If we didn't have two kinds of beauty

Laozi said: Control your body, cultivate your spirit. Regulate yourself and live at leisure. Eat and drink in moderation, harmonize enjoyment and anger, balance movement and stillness. Make it impossible for evil to enter you.

What appears attractive on the outside can wound you on the inside.

If you hold to your passions, you will harm your spirit. Notice that attractiveness blocks what is true. Evil will make you forget what is virtuous in a flash and it will firmly trap your inner nature. You will forget what has happened before you walk a hundred paces and your body will be consumed.

Therefore, beautiful arrows will pierce you to the bone. Luxuriant branches and leaves will harm the roots. If only the world did not have these two kinds of beauty!

Wenzi, "Talismanic Words" Ⓣ

48 | Not recognizing what a sage is

A high minister of Shang met Confucius and said: "Are you a sage?"

"I don't dare to call myself a sage. I am only someone who's learned a great deal and have some understanding," said Confucius.

"Were the Three Sovereigns sages?"

41

"The Three Sovereigns were excellent, trustworthy, wise, and brave. Whether they were sages or not, I cannot say."

"What about the Five Emperors then?"

"The Five Emperors were excellent, trustworthy, wise, and brave. Whether they were sages or not, I still cannot say."

"So were the Three Sovereigns sages?"

"The Three Sovereigns were excellent, trustworthy, wise, and brave because of their eras. Whether they would have been sages otherwise cannot be known."

The high minister of Shang grew agitated. "Then who can be a sage?"

Confucius noticed this shift but remained calm. "There may be a people who live to the west who have a sage among them. He does not try to rule them, and yet there is no disorder. He seldom speaks, but he is always trustworthy. He never changes how he lives. All the people are pure and earnest, and no one vies for fame. Should we doubt that he's a sage? The people don't even know whether to really call him a sage or not."

The high minister of Shang was silent, but in his heart, he said: "Confucius is trying to cheat me!"

Liezi, "Confucius" ⓣ

49 | For the sake of self-sufficient people

Laozi said: Food is the foundation of people; people are the foundation of a country. Therefore, a sovereign must act with heaven's natural order above, the conditions of the geography below, and must make use of the strength of the people in between. For everyone's lives to have long success, all living things must be allowed to grow and flourish.

In spring, the withered is renewed; in summer, we receive abundant fruit; in fall, we harvest vegetables; in winter, we gather firewood. All these are the people's resources, used to relieve weariness and distributed to each mouth to stave off death.

The laws of the Early Kings prohibited taking from the people as if taking fish from a pond, or burning forests before hunting, or killing beasts as jackals do. One was not to snare every rabbit in the field nor drag a net for every animal or fish in the waters. Eagles and falcons were not to be shot, bird nets were not to be spread in the marshes, the grasses and trees were not to be mowed down, hatchets were not to chop down entire mountain forests, fields were not to be burned before the insects had hibernated, pregnant animals were not to be harmed, fledglings and eggs were not to be sought, fish shorter than a foot were not be caught, and livestock younger than a year were not to be eaten.

All living things breathe in and exhale vapor.

This is the reason why the Early Kings took time to cultivate and prepare the Tao of a rich country that benefitted the people—instead of depending on what they saw with their eyes or paced off with their feet. In their desire to benefit the people, they never overlooked what was in their hearts: a self-sufficient people.

Wenzi, "Superior Benevolence" ⓣ

50 | Fasting of the heart

Yan Hui said, "I haven't been able to make progress. May I ask you what I should do?"

Confucius replied: "Fast. I'll tell you how to do it, but once I do, will you think it easy? Treat it lightly and bright heaven won't approve."

"My family is poor. We have had no wine, no pungent root vegetables, and no meat for many months. Could that be considered fasting?"

"This is the fasting one does before sacrificial ceremonies, but it is not fasting in the heart."

"May I ask, then, what is fasting in the heart?"

"It's having a single will. Don't just listen with your ears, listen with your heart. Don't just listen with your heart, listen with your breath.

"Listening stops with the ears. The heart stops upon recognition. The breath is empty and waits on all things. Only Tao gathers in emptiness. That emptiness is the fasting of the heart."

Zhuangzi, "The Human World" ⓣ

51 | Cultivate yourself

When you see what's good, examine yourself and cultivate the same. When you see what's bad, examine yourself, anxious that you might be the same. If you find goodness in yourself, commend yourself and hold to that goodness. If you find badness in yourself, reproach yourself and take it as your shortcoming.

Therefore, whoever correctly criticizes me is my teacher. Whoever supports me is my friend. But whoever flatters and inveigles me is my betrayer. Therefore, a noble one exalts his teachers and loves his friends, but avoids betrayers. They love goodness without end, and can accept admonishment and learn. Even if they didn't want to improve, they still would.

The inferior person is the opposite. They are disorderly and hate to be criticized. Although they are not, they still want others to regard them as worthy. They have hearts like a tiger or a wolf, conduct themselves like beasts, and they hate for anyone to think of them as traitorous. They favor those who flatter and inveigle them, and they dispute with those who admonish them. They laugh at cultivating correctness, and they consider it a loss to arrive at loyalty. Even if they don't want it, they still will be destroyed.

Xunzi, "Cultivating Oneself" ©

52 | The four mistakes in learning

There are four mistakes
a student makes when learning
that a teacher must know:

>trying to learn too much;

>trying to learn too little;

>trying to make everything easy;

>and trying to quit.

In all four cases
the heart will be scattered.
You must first know your heart.
Only then can you correct such mistakes.

Book of Rites, "Xue Ji" ©

53 | The four faults of governance

Zizhang asked: "What are the Four Faults?"

"Not educating people and executing them—this is called cruel.

"To search them without warning—this is called brutal.

"To be late to give orders and then setting a short time limit—this is called treacherous.

"To be stingy in rewarding people—this is called incompetent."

Analects, "Yao Yue" ©

Laozi said: To reach at a great and all-encompassing form-lessness is simplicity. To reach a greatness that is beyond measure is Tao.

Accordingly, heaven is round without needing a compass, and earth is square without needing a ruler. We may speak of eternity as proceeding from ancient times to today or discuss the universe in terms of the four directions as well as up and down. Yet the Tao is within all of this, without anyone being able to understand where it is.

Therefore, without looking far, you cannot speak of the great. If you don't have extensive knowledge, you can't arrive at an opinion. Those of Tao let things be open and there is no blaming one another. Thus, the recorded laws of the Three Sovereigns and the Five Emperors may have varied, but they were all the same in gaining the hearts of the people.

We may refer to the compass, square, and hooked line, but we are referring to the tools of a skill rather than the skill itself. So a master cannot pluck an instrument that lacks its strings, nor can a student play sad music on a lone string. In the first case, the reason is the lack of strings, not the instrument. In the second case, the apprentice can play no believably sad music.

When it comes to a harmonious spirit that travels from heart to hand to release its ideas, to write of the spirit, or to speak of love in the form of the strings of a musical instrument—this is a skill that a parent cannot teach to a child and a child cannot receive from a parent. The Tao of it cannot be passed on to others.

That's why reduction is sovereign over form and silence is the master of sound.

Wenzi, "Natural" ⊤

55 | Let music rule your heart

If you would be a cultivated person, you should always behave properly and have music. Music will make your heart peaceful. Your heart will be easy, straight, loving, and forgiving, and your life will be rich. That will bring joy, and joy will bring serenity.

Deep serenity means being completely with heaven. Heaven is the spirit. Heaven needs no explanation, and you can rely on it completely. The spirit has no anger and no aggression. All this can happen if you let music rule your heart.

If you behave properly, you will be honored in your community and you'll be seen as rigorous and powerful. But if you lack harmony and joy, meanness and falsity will enter your heart, you will be shunned by your community, and indifference and laziness will be in your heart.

Thus, let music move you inwardly. Move outwardly with the proper behavior.

Music is the ultimate peaceful harmony. Proper behavior is the ultimate way to act. If you have internal harmony with

proper outer behavior, then people will be glad to see you, and there will be no conflicts. Others will be moved when they look at you and they will not hesitate to be with you. As long as you are virtuous, bright, and lively inside, people will listen to you. If all your outer actions are reasonable, people will cooperate with you.

There's a saying: "Tao combines proper behavior with music. That rights all wrongs, and all difficulties will vanish."

Book of Rites, "Yue Ji" ©

56 | The secret of music

I use musical notes that are brisk. I let them move in a natural order. They come forth like a great rush of water, with the profusion of a bursting thicket or as forest music without shapes. They spread without trace, then fall dark and silent.

Their movements are limitless. They rise from deep obscurity. Some call that death. Some call that life. Some call that the fruit. Some call that the flower. Moving, flowing, scattering, shifting, they do not obey any orthodox sounds.

The world might question that and ask the sages to investigate. But the sages are intelligent in their emotions and have passed through life. The heavenly opportunities are not enormous. The five notes must be prepared. Only then can you have divine music that can delight the heart without needing any words.

49

That is why it is said of the *Eulogy of the Lord of Yan:* "Listen, and you will hear no sound. Look and you will see no shape. Yet it fully fills heaven and earth. It envelopes all six directions."

If you want to hear, but don't comprehend, you'll be confused.

Zhuangzi, "The Movement of Heaven" ⓣ

57 | Why isn't following Tao easier?

Gongsun Chou said: "Your Tao is lofty and beautiful. But it's as hard to learn as it is to ascend to heaven. It seems unattainable. Why not make it easier so that many people could practice it each day?"

Mengzi replied: "A great carpenter does not change for incompetent workers or do away with the marking line. The legendary archer Yi did not change his methods for the sake of a clumsy archer. A noble one draws his bow, does not need to shoot, and still leaps to the mark. The noble one stands in the center of Tao for those who can follow."

Mengzi, "Jin Xin I" ©

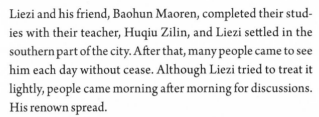

58 | To know without knowing

Liezi and his friend, Baohun Maoren, completed their studies with their teacher, Huqiu Zilin, and Liezi settled in the southern part of the city. After that, many people came to see him each day without cease. Although Liezi tried to treat it lightly, people came morning after morning for discussions. His renown spread.

A man named Nanguozi had lived in a neighboring house for twenty years. He never came to visit. Whenever they passed each other in the street, he didn't so much as glance at Liezi. The many visitors had no doubt that the two must have become adversaries.

One day, a visitor from Chu asked Liezi about this: "Is there some conflict between you and Nanguozi?"

"Nanguozi has the appearance of fullness, but his heart is empty. His ears hear nothing. His eyes see nothing. His mouth does not speak. His heart recognizes nothing. His body is never aroused. Why is all that? Let's try to see him together and find out."

Some forty followers went with Liezi to call on Nanguozi. But when they arrived, they could not believe it: the man's soul seemed gone. People glanced at Liezi. Nanguozi's spirit and body seemed separated and he looked like a statue. The crowd was dumbfounded.

Nanguozi suddenly awoke and pointed his finger at the gathering. He gestured at everyone, including those at the back. "You are arrogant men who only want to monopolize

THE WAY OF HEART & BEAUTY

happiness for yourselves." The crowd was shocked. They angrily went back to Liezi's house and questioned him.

Liezi said to them: "Someone with realized intentions has no need to speak. Someone with advanced wisdom doesn't need words. If you don't hear him speak, he is still talking. If you don't see his knowledge, he is still wise.

"He speaks without speaking, and he knows without needing to investigate. Mere speech and mere knowledge don't lead to true speech or wisdom. The mere absence of speech or the mere absence of wisdom are also worthless. Why should you be shocked or doubt this?"

Liezi, "Confucius" Ⓣ

59 | Buddha holds a flower

When the Most Honored One, Shakyamuni Buddha, was at a gathering on Mount Grdhrakuta, he held up a flower before the assembly.

Everyone was silent.

Only Mahakashyapa broke into a broad smile.

The Most Honored One said: "I have the True Dharma Eye, the Marvelous Heart of Nirvana, the Ultimate Essence Beyond Essence, the Subtle Dharma Gate, and that which is independent of words and transmitted outside doctrine. I give them all over to Mahakashyapa."

Wumenguan, Case 6 Ⓑ

60 | Beautiful words are sold at market

Among the ten thousand things,
Tao is the most profound.
It is the treasure of good people,
and the protector of bad people.

Beautiful words are sold at the market.
Noble deeds can be presented as a gift.
Even bad people are not abandoned.

A king is enthroned as the son of heaven
and appoints his three ministers.
The nobles may present their jade disks
and parade their teams of horses,
but it's not as good as presenting Tao.

Why did the ancient prize Tao so much?
Was it not because:
it could be had by any who sought it,
and that the guilty could find forgiveness in it?
That is why it is the treasure of the world.

Daodejing, 62 ⓣ

61 | In beautiful solitude

In middle-age, I found the right Tao
and I made my home at South Mountain.
I rise, and wander the land in beautiful solitude.
Problems overcome, I know the empty self.
I walk and reach the point where the stream begins,
sit and watch for the moment when clouds rise.
Sometimes I happen to meet an old woodsman.
We talk and laugh, with no hurry to go.

Wang Wei (699–759), "Zhongnan Mountain Retreat" Ⓑ

62 | Virtue will be your beauty

Nie Que went to Bei Yi to ask about Tao. Bei Yi said: "If you keep your body as you should, the harmony of heaven will come to you. Absorb your wisdom, standardize your measures, and the gods will come to live with you. Take virtue as your beauty, and take Tao as your home. You will have the look of a new-born calf without needing to seek for who you are!"

Before his words were done, Nie Que fell asleep.

Bei Yi was greatly pleased. He walked away, singing:

"With a body like a withered tree trunk,
a heart like dead ash,
realizing solid wisdom,
with no need to grasp at the original self.
Between darkness and night,

without a heart of intention, without schemes,
who could be that kind of person?"

Zhuangzi, "Knowledge While Roaming in the North"

63 | The art of nourishing the heart

This is the art of regulating the breath and nourishing the heart:

When one's blood and breath run with excessive vigor and strength, neutralize and blend them with softness. When one's thoughts become overly deep, then unify them with ease and goodness. When one is ferocious, brave, bold, and stubborn, then reform by submitting to Tao. When one rushes toward expedient benefits, then regulate with measured movements. When one is too narrow, cramped, and small, then broaden with expansive greatness. When one is overly humble, sluggish, or covetous for gain, then resist with high aspirations. When one falls into vulgarity or dissoluteness, then force it away with teachers and friends. When one is neglectful or careless, then illuminate by thinking of calamity. When one is foolishly righteous or excessively honest, combine rites and music and think of what's right.

In summation, in the art of regulating the breath and nourishing the heart, nothing is more direct than ritual. Nothing is more important than having a teacher. Nothing is more spiritual than holding to one excellence. This is called the art of regulating the breath and nourishing the heart.

Xunzi, "Cultivating Oneself"

55

Laozi said: Those who keep Tao guide the people. In all affairs that happen they are compliant. As all things move, they follow. The ten thousand things change unforced. The hundred affairs develop without any confusion.

Thus, the Tao is empty and void; even and easy; peaceful and tranquil; soft and subtle; clean, pure, plain, and simple. These are firm images of Tao.

Empty and void is the abode of Tao.

Even and easy is the simplicity of Tao.

Peaceful and tranquil is the reflection of Tao.

Soft and subtle is the function of Tao.

Reversal is the constancy of Tao. Softness is the strength of Tao. Subtlety is the power of Tao. Cleanliness, purity, plainness, and simplicity are the trunk of Tao.

If you are empty within, then you are unburdened. If you are even, then your heart will be unbothered. Once you are unburdened by weaknesses and desires, you will reach emptiness. Once you have neither likes nor dislikes, you will reach evenness. Once you are unified and unchanging, you will reach tranquility. Once you are not mixed up in things, you will reach purity. Once you are neither sad nor elated, you will reach virtue.

Wenzi, "The Source of Tao" Ⓣ

Zhaozhou asked his teacher, Nanquan Puyan (c. 748–c. 835), "What is Tao?"

"The ordinary heart is Tao."

"Can I go toward it or not?"

"If you try by thinking, it will elude you."

"But if I don't think about it, how will I know Tao?"

"Tao is not proven by knowing. It is not disproven by not-knowing. Knowing is delusion. Not-knowing is confusion. When you have truly attained the Tao beyond intellectual proof, it will be like a great emptiness, as big and open as a vast cavern. How can you seize it by thinking of what *is* or *is-not?*"

With these words, Zhaozhou reached enlightenment.

WUMEN SAID: "Nanquan met Zhaozhou's question by collapsing and melting away like ice. He did not clear away the obstruction. Even after Zhaozhou had his realization, he will have to continue for another thirty years before he really has it."

WUMEN'S VERSE:

The spring has hundreds of flowers, the autumn has the
    moon.

The summer has cool breezes, the winter has snow.

If useless matters don't hang in your heart and head,

you will have the best seasons of this human world.

Wumenguan, Case 19 Ⓑ

THE WAY OF HEART & BEAUTY

The True Person of ancient times was not giddy over life and was unafraid of death. They entered life without delight and they left without protest. They went briskly, they came briskly, and that was all.

They did not forget their beginning, and they did not complain about their ending. If they received something, they were thankful, and if they missed something, they just returned to their path. That's called "not giving up Tao in your heart and not trying to push heaven."

Therefore, their hearts were steady, their looks were calm, and their foreheads were unlined. For them, bitter cold was as mild as autumn, hot weather was like spring, and their emotions passed from one to the next like the turning of the four seasons. They felt that all things had a place—and yet they didn't think of that as limited.

In the past, even if the sages went to war, they would rather have lost a nation than have lost the hearts of the people. They brought benefit and brilliance to everything and all creatures without preferential love for anyone.

Zhuangzi, "The Great and Honored Master" ⓣ

67 | As long as your heart is at peace

Cultivate purpose and intention and you will disregard wealth and prestige. When you are heavily concerned with Tao and righteousness, you'll regard kings and dukes lightly.

If you emphasize the inner, then outer things will be light. A saying goes: "The noble one makes things into servants. The inferior person makes servants into things." That is what's meant. If your body must labor, but your heart is at peace, then do so. If benefit is slight but the righteousness is great, then do so.

Completely serving a king who causes chaos is not as good as obediently serving an impoverished king. Therefore, a good farmer never fails to plant, even in drought. An excellent merchant never misses going to market, even if there have been losses. The scholar and the noble one never neglects Tao, even if they are poor.

Xunzi, "Cultivating Oneself" ©

68 | What is Buddha?

A monk asked Mazu, "What is Buddha?"
"No heart, no Buddha."

WUMEN SAID: "If you can see this, you have learned the whole."

WUMEN'S VERSE:

If you meet a swordsperson on the road, you must
    present a sword.
Don't offer a poem if you don't meet a poet.
To those you meet, speak of one-third.
You cannot give the whole in a single slice.

Wumen Huikai (1183–1260), *The Mountain Pass of No-Gate*, Case 33 Ⓑ

69 | Subduing through excellence

Those who would subdue people through their own
    "excellence"
have yet to subdue anyone.

But if you used excellence to nurture people instead,
then the whole world would be subdued.

No one has become ruler of all under heaven
without subdued hearts.

It has never happened.

Mengzi, "Li Lou II" Ⓒ

Yan Hui asked Zhongni: "When Mengsun Cai's mother died, he wailed but showed no tears. He did not seem to grieve in his heart. He displayed no sorrow at the funeral. He showed none of these three signs, and yet he was known throughout the state of Lu for organizing an excellent funeral. Can someone really achieve such a reputation without factual support? I find this strange."

"Mengsun did the best he could," Confucius replied. "Although he was advanced in wisdom, there were some levels he couldn't achieve.

"He got enough for himself, but ultimately, he didn't understand life and death. He did not know what came first, and what came after. If he is to be transformed into another being, he simply waits without knowing how he's changing! Besides, while he's in the middle of transformation, he might not even know that the change has started! Or if nothing seems to be happening to him, he won't even know when change has occurred.

"You and I are dreaming, and we have not yet begun to wake!"

Zhuangzi, "The Great and Honored Master" Ⓣ

71 | Your heart will be devoted and true

Keep a respectful and reverent bearing, and your heart will be devoted and true. Use ritual and righteousness as your method with a feeling of love for all people. Then you can journey across the world, and even if you're besieged by barbarians, no one will fail to value you.

Take the lead even in matters of labor and hardship. Give way and let pleasant matters be plentiful. Be completely honest, sincere, and true; be restrained, protective, and meticulous. Then you can journey across the world, and even if you're besieged by barbarians, no one will regard you as lowly.

Xunzi, "Cultivating Oneself" ©

72 | Trying to see autumn fur

Eyes will go blind trying to see a hair of autumn fur.
Ears will go deaf trying to hear the flight of a mosquito.
A mouth will go giddy trying to discern differences in river
       water.
A nose will recoil smelling what's scorched and rotten.
A body will grow turgid constantly running after pleasure.
A heart will go mad trying to know right and wrong.

Therefore, if people don't reason things out,
they will never reach realization.

Liezi, "Confucius" ⓣ

73 | Beauty to match heaven and earth

Laozi said: The great Tao acts through nonaction. Nonaction means never possessing.

Never possessing means never being static. Never to be static means to abide in the formless.

Formlessness is to be motionless. To be motionless means silence.

Silence means a stillness without sound or shape. To be without sound or shape means to see the unseen and hear the unheard.

This is called subtle. This is called to reach the spiritual: "Continuous as existence, this means the root of heaven and earth."

Tao is silent. Therefore, the sages are powerful in form—one sentence serves to name all the Tao of heaven and earth. The great is formed because it had a root when small. The profuse is possible because of slight beginnings. The Son of Heaven is chosen by heaven and earth in order to support the ten thousand things.

When achievements and virtue reach greatness, power and fame reach great value. The beauty of both kinds of virtue match heaven and earth.

Therefore, one must never oppose the great Tao. It is the mother of all under heaven.

Wenzi, "Absolute Sincerity" ⑦

A monk asked Xing Yangran, "The Buddha of Universally Pervading Superlative Wisdom sat in meditation for ten kalpas and yet did not attain full Buddhahood. How could that be?"

"Your question answers itself."

"He meditated so long, why could he not attain the Tao of Buddhism?"

"Because he did not become a Buddha."

WUMEN SAID: "I allow that the barbarian is aware, but I do not allow that the barbarian understands. The average person who seems to know is a sage. The sage who understands is an average person."

WUMEN'S VERSE:
Sooner free your body than your heart.
Free your heart and your body will have no worries.
If the body and heart are both freed, why would you
    need
gods and immortals to grant you a title?

Wumenguan, Case 9 Ⓑ

75 | How to bring order to the world

Tian Gen (Heavenly Root) was traveling in Yinyang (Abundant Yang). He came to Smartweed Waters, where he encountered Wumingren (Nameless Person) and said: "May I please ask: what can be done to bring order to the world?"

"Go away!" said Wumingren. "How rude of you to ask such a difficult question! I simply do as the Maker of all beings does. I am satisfied to ride a bird, fly beyond the six directions, travel to where nothing exists, and linger in wild limitlessness. Why should you ask me about 'bringing order to the world' and agitating my heart?"

But Tian Gen asked again. So Wumingren said, "Let your heart wander in the limpid. Unite your energies without passion. Conform to the nature of all beings. Reject pride and selfishness. Then there will be order in the world."

Zhuangzi, "The Course of Emperors and Kings" ⓣ

76 | The greatest strength in the world

This is how a ruler heard of a strong man named Gongyibo.

The report of this powerful man came to the court of King Zhuan of Zhou (r. 827–782 BCE), who sent gifts with an invitation. Gongyibo arrived in court. But the king judged the man's appearance to be timid and weak and he declared the doubts and questions in his heart: "Can you even manage the strength of a woman?"

"I am strong enough to break the legs off a spring katydid, or pluck the wings off an autumn cicada."

The king angrily leapt to his feet: "I am strong enough to strip the hide from a rhinoceros with my bare hands! I can drag nine bulls by their tails! Your weakness offends me! Any woman can break the legs of a katydid or pluck the wings off a cicada, but how could you have a strength heard throughout the world?"

Gongyibo paused for a long time, went back to his mat, and bowed. "It's right that his majesty should ask, and so your subject will dare to respond. My teacher's name was Shang Qiu. His strength was unrivaled throughout the world and yet no one in his entire family ever knew he had it—and he never had to use it. Your subject decided to follow this way until death.

"My teacher told me this: 'People want to see, but don't look. The want to peer at others, but they don't observe them. They want to obtain, but they get nothing. They fail to cultivate themselves. Therefore, to learn through observation, you must first see. To learn aurally, you must be able to hear the slightest clink of a glass. Once you can detect inner change, external situations are easy and there are no difficulties. However, if you try to make a name for yourself instead, you will never realize Tao.'

"Now, if your subject's strength has become known to your majesty, then I must have violated what my teacher said to me. If I should become known for my abilities, it shouldn't be because of how I carry my strength. It should be because of how I use strength. Otherwise, strength is just another load to carry."

Liezi, "Confucius" Ⓣ

77 | He wanted to push all evil from his heart

Bo Yi would not serve a ruler who was corrupt, nor would he associate with anyone who could not be a good friend. He would refuse to stand in the court of a wicked ruler, and he would not converse with evil persons. If he were to stand in a wicked ruler's court, or if he spoke with an evil person, he would have seen it as being gloriously dressed in official robes and cap only to sit in utter misery. He only wanted to push all evil from his own heart.

Mengzi, "Gong Sun Chou I" ©

78 | The teacher who had no feet

A man named Wang Tai had lost both feet. He lived in the state of Lu. Seeing that he had as many disciples as Zhongni himself, Chang Ji (Constant Seasons) went to discuss this with his teacher, Zhongni.

"Although both of Wang Tai's feet have been amputated," Chang Ji asked, "he has many disciples in Lu, as you do. But when he stands, he doesn't teach. When he sits, he holds no discussions. When students go to him, they are empty. When they come back, they are full. Is it possible to teach like that without words? What's more, can someone whose body is not intact have a whole heart? What kind of person can he be?"

"This master is a sage," replied Zhongni. "I have neglected to study with him sooner. If I would take him as a teacher, everyone should, even beyond the borders of Lu. I would have everyone in the world follow him."

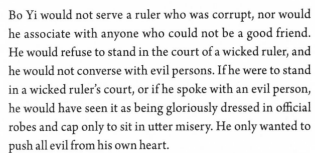

"He has lost both feet, but he's addressed as Venerable Wang. That implies that he's far from ordinary. How does he use his heart so unusually?"

"Life and death loom large, but they don't deter him. If heaven and earth were to turn over and fall in disaster, it would cause him no loss. He is clear and has no delusions. He obeys the ordained changes of all things, and he keeps to that lineage."

"What do you mean?"

"When we examine things, we look at differences—the differences between the liver and gallbladder, for instance, or the differences between the states of Chu and Yue. Then we look at the similarities of things, and we see the ten thousand things as one. He does the same, except that he does not gain knowledge through his ears and eyes, but through a dynamic heart that is always in virtuous harmony. When he looks at the unity of all things, he does not look at what has been lost. If he looks at the loss of his feet, he regards it only as leaving behind some dirt."

"So he acts within himself," said Chang Ji. "Maybe he knows his own heart. Maybe in his heart of hearts, he is constant. But why do others make so much of him?"

"People don't look use flowing water for a mirror. They look into still water. Only that stillness can hold any kind of reflection. Of all the things that this earth holds, only the pine and cedar stand out for being green in all seasons. Of all that heaven has held, only Yao and Shun stood out as being

the most correct. Because they had the fortune to live correctly, only they could make the lives of others correct.

"For example, musicians begin by sounding the right pitch; the fearlessness of a single warrior can make a difference when thrown in among nine armies. If a single pitch or one hero can have such an impact, it should be the same for an official in this world. They who must serve all creatures resides in their own bones, is attentive and observant, understands as soon as they see—and their heart never dies! If such a person were to one day rise above the mediocre, all people would rise together too! Who is willing to do that?"

Zhuangzi, "The Seal of Virtue" ⊤

79 | Beauty is harmony

The Tao of heaven and earth is ultimately about reversal. Increase follows decrease. Therefore, a sage addresses both degeneracy and reform, trying to resolve all endeavors even more. The beauty of that is to achieve harmony. The loss of that brings on authoritarianism.

Therefore, the sages speak of Tao in this way: Do not fail to cultivate ritual and righteousness. If honor or shame are not established, if the people have no sense of honor or shame, then there can be no governance. If there is no knowledge of ritual and righteousness, then laws will not be correct. If no higher good abolishes disgrace, no one will be directed by ritual and righteousness. Without correct laws, there cannot be order. Without knowing ritual and righteousness, there cannot be active laws. Laws can kill, but they cannot make people filial or teach them to be filial. You can punish people from stealing, but you cannot coerce them into being incorruptible.

Wenzi, "Superior Ritual" Ⓣ

80 | The root is not beautiful

Laozi said: The noble one stays with the fundamental teachings. The petty person seeks their own beneficence basically out of self-interest. The noble one benefits from their own meritorious deeds.

Each should be taught according to what suits them, as long as communications and exercises are easy to absorb and lead to reaching Tao. People have many wishes that undermine righteousness, and many worries that trouble their wisdom.

Therefore, rule a country through happiness and survive. Rule a country tyrannically and happiness will be gone. Just as water flows downward and covers vast areas, the ruler must flow downward to the officials and intelligent people. The ruler must never vie with the officials if governance is to be as pervasive as Tao.

Thus, the ruler should be the root. The officials should be the branches and leaves. The root may not be beautiful, but the branches and leaves will be magnificent.

And yet: it's never been done.

Wenzi, "Abstruse Understanding" Ⓣ

81 | Feeling each passing moment

The sun endures, the moon is so;
Why should they repeatedly set?
My heart is as sad
as unwashed clothes.
Wordlessly, I ponder that,
unable to spread wings and fly.

Classic of Poetry, "Bo Zhou" ©

82 | The "illness" of being a sage

Long Shu (Uncle Dragon) questioned Wen Zhi (Sincere Language): "I've heard you have some skill. I have an illness. Can you cure it?"

"Once I hear of it, it would be my command," Wen Zhi replied. "But you have to tell me about it and let me examine you."

"I am prominent in my village, but it brings me no sense of glory. If I were to be accused before the whole country, it would bring me no embarrassment. When I gain possessions, it brings me no joy. When I lose, it brings me no sadness. I see life as being the same as death. I see wealth as being the same as poverty. I see people as being the same as pigs. I see myself as being the same as all other people. I see my family's house as being the same as a wayfarer's hut. I see my village as being the same as all the nomadic countries abroad.

In view of all these details, then, I've lost all urge for rank and reward, lost all fear of penalties and punishments, find that abundance and decline, as well as gain and loss, make no difference to me, and that the fluctuations between grief and joy don't matter to me anymore. I no longer care about the affairs of my country or king; the relationships of family and friends; dealing with my wife and children; or managing my servants. What kind of illness is this? Can you cure it?"

Wen Zhi asked Long Shu to stand up and turn around. He looked at his friend from the back and said, "Well! I see that your heart, sir, has one square inch that's empty. You're on your way to becoming a sage! However, while your heart and six of your openings are flowing clear, one opening is still clogged. Now, to become a sage means having your kind of illness. I wouldn't use my skill to 'cure' you!"

Liezi, "Confucius" ⓣ

83 | The noble ones and the inferior persons

The noble ones are the opposite of inferior persons. Noble ones with big hearts honor heaven through Tao, and with small (i.e., careful) hearts regulate themselves with reverent righteousness. If smart, they are enlightened to every category of thing. If yet unlearned, they scrupulously and honestly follow the right standards. If they see employment, then they are reverent and reserved. If they see dismissal, then they are respectful and controlled. If happy, they are harmonious and thoughtful. If sad, they are calm and logi-

cal. If successful, they are refined and enlightened. If poor they remain restrained and thorough.

But inferior persons are not like this. If they try to act with a big heart, they are slow and brutal. With small hearts, they run to lewdness and dissolution. If smart, they become robbers who slowly steal everything. If yet unlearned, they are toxic thieves who sow chaos. If they see employment, they make deals and are arrogant. If they see dismissal, they turn hateful and dangerous.

The saying goes: "In both cases, the noble ones advance. In both cases, the inferior persons fail." This shows what that means.

Xunzi, "Never Improper" ©

84 | The leadership of enlightened kings

Yang Ziju met with Lao Dan (Laozi). "There is someone who is direct, tireless, energetic, strong, substantial, broad, highly bright, and they never stop learning of Tao. Could you compare them to one of the enlightened kings?"

"Such a person would seem to be a sage," Lao Dan replied. "But subject them to change, thwart their skills, work their bodies to exhaustion, and you will threaten their hearts.

"Men hunt tigers and leopards for their skins. They tether apes, monkey, and dogs to mats for their agility or abilities. If we view your question that way, would a person still be like one of the enlightened sages?"

Ziju shifted uncomfortably and said, "Let me ask about the leadership of enlightened kings."

"The merit of the enlightened kings spread to all under heaven, but they ask nothing for themselves. They transform the conditions for all beings, and yet the people are unaware of their work. There is no drive for fame. They make all living beings happy. Where they chose to stand cannot be known, and they roam in nonexistence."

Zhuangzi, "The Normal Course for Emperors and Kings" ⑦

85 | A heart of integrity

When it comes to a noble one nourishing the heart, there's no greater good than integrity. Without it, one cannot carry out one's duties. With it, one can preserve one's benevolence and act with righteousness. If you have a heart of integrity, you'll embody it. If you embody it, you'll be spiritual. If you're spiritual, you'll be able to effect change.

A heart of integrity acts righteously and is orderly. Orderliness leads to enlightenment. Enlightenment leads to being able to transform all. Transformation and change, adapting and flourishing, are called heavenly virtue.

Heaven does not speak, yet people infer its height. Earth does not speak, yet people infer its thickness. The four seasons do not speak, and yet all the people learn their rhythm. All these are constant because they have integrity.

The noble one is the ultimate in integrity. They silently set an example. They give to others without receiving special favors. They are powerful without resorting to anger. Everyone obeys their orders because the noble one acts with steadfast care.

The Tao of such goodness means that without integrity, there is no steadfastness. Without steadfastness, there is no embodiment. Without embodiment, people will not follow you even if you try to put it in your heart, your face, and your words. They won't follow you because they will be suspicious.

Heaven and earth are great, but without integrity, they could not bring forth the ten thousand things. The sage is wise, but without integrity, they would not be able to bring change to the people. Parent and child love each other, but without integrity they would drift apart. King and officials are exalted, but without integrity, they would be despised.

So integrity is what a noble one should guard the most. It is the root of all government affairs. If they maintain that, all levels of society will also come to the same point.

If you grasp it, you will attain it. If you let go, you will lose it. If you grasp and attain it, it becomes light. If it is light, then you will be steadfast in action. If you are steadfast in action without letting go, then you will improve. If you improve and develop your talents, if you keep moving forward for a long time without going back to where you started, then you will be changed.

Xunzi, "Never Improper" ©

86 | Every idea brings immediate response

As soon as an idea arises in your heart
heaven and earth will surely know.
If good and bad were without retribution
then heaven and earth would be partial.

Wu Cheng'en (1500–1582), *Journey to the West* Ⓛ

87 | The method is concealment

The True Persons maximize themselves but minimize the world. They value controlling themselves instead of controlling others. They don't let their harmony slip away with things. They don't let desire confuse their emotions. They hide their name and surname. The method of those with Tao is concealment, while those without Tao is visibility.

Do by not-doing. Endeavor through no-endeavors. Know through not-knowing. Carry heaven's Tao in you. Embrace heaven's heart. Exhale and inhale yin and yang. Expel the old and take in the new. Close together with yin. Open together with yang. Roll and open with hardness and softness. Bow down and rise up with yin and yang.

Keep your heart the same with heaven. Keep your body with Tao. There is no joy, no bitterness, no happiness, no anger. The ten thousand things are profoundly united. There is nothing wrong and there is nothing right.

When people fall ill, it's due to the harshness of cold and hot, dry and damp. When we examine them physically, we find that their spirit is also affected. Their spirit falls ill and their faculties of enjoyment, anger, thought, and interest suffer. The spirit can become exhausted even if the body still has strength left.

Therefore, the True Person uses their heart to prop up their feelings and to soothe their spirit. By supporting both the body and the spirit, they can have a new start. Then they sleep without disturbing dreams and wake without worry.

Wenzi, "The Source of Tao" ⓣ

88 | The teaching that has not yet been preached

A monk asked Nanquan: "Have any of the Buddha's teachings not been preached to the people?"

"There have."

"What teachings that have not yet been preached?"

"It is not the heart. It is not Buddha. It is not things."

Wumenguan, Case 27 ⓑ

89 | Comparing horses and people

Horses live on the open plains, graze on grass, and drink water. When they're happy, they rub their necks against one another. When angry, they turn away and kick. Horses know how to do this by instinct.

But if we fit them with a bit and a bridle that curves in a crescent over their foreheads, the horses are unwilling to wear them. They bend their necks, buck for a long time, try to slip the bit from their mouths, and pull the reins away. If a horse learns to resist like this, it is the crime of Bo Le.

In the era of He Xu, people lived in their homes without knowing what they were doing. They walked without knowing where they were going. When they ate, they were glad; they slapped their bellies and went on.

The sages came and distorted people with rites and music as they tried to make everyone in the world correct. They spread ideas of benevolence and righteousness to every district and tried to subdue the hearts of everyone in the world.

People began to paw and creep because they now knew of being "good." They grappled with each other to bring back benefits for themselves. It was impossible to stop them.

That is the folly of the sages.

Zhuangzi, "Horse Hooves" ⑦

90 | They are methodical

Although the noble one has an honored position, they keep a reverent purpose. Their heart is small, while Tao is great. As a consequence, they listen and look at what is near. They hear and see what is far. How can they do that? They carry this skill: they can consider the personalities of a thousand people, or ten thousand, as easily as one person.

From the beginning of heaven and earth until today, from the Tao of the Early Kings to that of the later kings, the noble one investigates the Tao of the Early Kings and analyzes what confronted them. The noble one discusses these issues with others.

They bow, but they are able to bring forth the controlling influence of the rites and of righteousness, separate the difference between right and wrong, gather together all that's crucial in the world, and bring order to all the people within the four seas, all the way to the last person. Thus, they hold with restraint, yet they fulfill their duties with greatness.

A five-inch square can set each corner of the world. The noble one can sense all the facts within the four seas without leaving home or hall—all because they are methodical.

Xunzi, "Never Improper" ©

91 | How to know everything

Confucius asked Laozi about Tao. Laozi replied: "Align your body. Unite your vision. Then heaven's harmony will arrive. Support your knowledge, standardize your tools. Then the spirits will come to dwell, virtue will suffuse your appearance, and Tao will remain with you.

"Gaze as if you're a newborn calf. Don't seek for causes. Make your body like a withered tree and your heart like dead ashes. Realize true knowledge instead of holding what's twisted and old. Restore the immensity of a heart that does not scheme with ill-intentions. If you understand all these points then what won't you know?"

Wenzi, "The Source of Tao" Ⓣ

92 | The heart knows beauty and truth

Among the people of Qi, no one speaks to the king about kindness and justice. Are they silent because they think that kindness and justice are not beautiful?

No, it's because their hearts say: "It's not enough just to talk about kindness and justice."

Mengzi, "Gong Sun Chou II" Ⓒ

93 | Do we need anyone to rule the world?

"If no one ruled the world," Cui Ji asked Lao Dan, "how could you pacify anyone's hearts?"

Lao Dan said: "Be careful not to meddle with people's hearts. When you force people's hearts into formation, they falter. If you let them advance, they rise. Alternating between rising and faltering restricts and corrupts.

Pliable and soft, then hard and strong; stiff and sharp enough to carve jade; hot and scorched with fire; cold and solid as ice; quick as an angry jerk; twice as calm as anything beyond the four seas; resting in the stillness of an abyss; hurtling like the regions of heaven; resolute, spirited, refusing to be bound—that is the human heart!

Zhuangzi, "At Profundity" ⓣ

94 | Everyone is angry with me

My sad heart is quiet but anxious:
everyone is angry with me.
I meet with many grievances,
receive not a few insults.
I think about all this silently
and awaken with my thrashing.

Classic of Poetry, "Bo Zhou" ©

95 | How to make a general lose heart

Even three armies can be robbed of their energy,
and a general can be made to lose heart.

A soldier's energy is keenest at dawn,
but it starts to flag by noon,
and it will retreat by dusk.

A good general therefore avoids using troops
when the enemy's energy is keenest,
and attacks as their energy recedes.
This is the study of energy.

Be orderly while they tarry in disorder;
be calm while they tarry in clamor;
be close while they tarry at a distance;
be at ease while they tarry in toil and struggle;
be full while they tarry in hunger.

This is the study of strength.

The Art of War, "Maneuvering" Ⓛ

96 | Once the heart sends out its feelings

Laozi said: One shout from a warrior can repel three armies
because it issues forth with sincerity. It may be loud but it is
harmonious, it conveys determination, and it certainly dis-
rupts troops.

82

Similarly, one need not leave one's seat in order to right the world or to find various situations for oneself. That's why we say that there is no place to arrive and no appearance to achieve. If there is no appearance to achieve, how can our feet fail to arrive at our destination?

Once the heart sends out its feelings, success takes shape. Once that essence is here, it has form and connects, and it illuminates in a short time.

Wenzi, "Sincerity" Ⓣ

97 | Wrap pure emptiness

Knots of grass issue from the fertile land:
their round masses wrap pure emptiness.
Mountain flowers drop before a remote hall
where people gather, free of worldly concerns.
Any such concerns have roots, even if they're unwanted,
so look into emptiness to be without distinctions.
Ten thousand sounds always have effects,
but silence is within the farthest and deepest noise.
The roots of our hearts' feelings are the same:
birds fly and leave no trace.

Liu Zongyuan (773–819), "The Chan Meditation Hall" Ⓑ

The bodies of sages seem to be completely wrapped and bound in precious silk—and yet they don't know it's so. It's a matter of their nature. They return to their inner impulses, and yet they are heaven's leaders. People follow them and so find their destinies.

Even in sorrow, the sages are wise, and they continue their activities in every season. How could they stop?

A sage is born beautiful. People are like mirrors, but if people made no mention of it, the sages wouldn't know of their own beauty. If sages learn of it, they act as if they did not know. If they hear of it, they act as if they did not hear.

Whatever a sage finds joyful has no end. Whatever people find good also has no end. It's all natural.

The sages love people. The people recognize the sage but if people made no mention of it, the sages wouldn't know that they love the people.

If the sages learn of it, they act as if they did not know. If they hear of it, they act as if they did not hear.

Whatever a sage loves has no end. Whatever people find safe also has no end. It's all natural.

Zhuangzi, "Zeyang" ⓣ

All people have these in common: when hungry, they want to eat; when cold, they want warmth; when they have worked hard, they want rest. They like what is beneficial and they hate what is harmful. People are born like that; they don't acquire it. Even Yu the Great or Jie the Wicked were the same.

Furthermore, the eyes distinguish white and black, beautiful and ugly. The ears distinguish between noise and music, clear and muffled. The mouth distinguishes between sour, salty, sweet, and bitter. The nose distinguishes between aromatic, fragrant, rancid, and fetid. Bones, body, skin, and reason distinguish between cold and hot, or between what will sicken or nourish. These abilities are also in-born, not acquired. It was the same for Yu or Jie.

Whether Yao or Yu, Jie or the Robber Zhi, laborer or craftsperson, farmer or merchant, everyone accumulates their abilities through concentration, error, practice, and habits. It comes from how they live, not what they have. They don't get it from nature. In this, Yu and Jie were also the same.

Compare the lasting glory of Yao and Yu to the lasting wickedness of Jie and Zhi; compare the lasting pleasures of Yao and Yu to the lasting labor of workers, craftspersons, farmers, or merchants—people's strength seems applied to becoming the latter rather than the former. Why?

Crudeness.

Yao and Yu were not born accomplished; they had to rise up, change, and complete themselves through long cultivation.

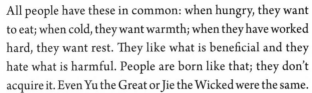

THE
WAY
OF
H
E
A
R
T
&
B
E
A
U
T
Y

They had to go through the entire process and only became perfect afterward.

When people are born, they are little. Without a teacher and method, they'll only seek the benefits of what they see and hear. When people are born, they are small. Again, if they encounter confusion in the world, then they become confused and vulgar people. This is inferiority added to inferiority, confusion following confusion. The noble one has no ability to achieve an opening of their inner selves for them.

Today, people care only for their mouths and bellies. How can they know of ritual and righteousness? How can they know of deference and yielding? What do they know of honesty, humility, and the cumulative effort? They just keep prattling on. They just keep eating to stuff themselves full.

If people have no teacher and no method, then their hearts are fixed only on their mouths and bellies.

Xunzi, "Never Improper" ©

100 | Cloud Commander and Vast Ignorance

Yun Jiang (Cloud Commander) was traveling in the east, passing by on a wisp of a breeze, when he encountered Hong Meng (Vast Ignorance). Hong Meng slapped his buttocks and skipped like a sparrow as he capered about.

Seeing this, Yun Jiang halted and said respectfully, "Elder, who are you? Why are you acting this way?"

Hong Meng didn't bother to stop. As he went on slapping his buttocks and hopping about, he said: "I'm traveling."

"I'd like to ask you a question."

Hong Meng looked up at him and said, "Shoo!"

Yun Jiang pressed on anyway: "Heaven's energy is not in harmony. Earth's energy is bottled up. The Six Energies are not in accord. The four seasons are irregular. Now, I want to balance the essence of those Six Energies so that all living things can flourish. How can I do that?"

Hong Meng slapped his buttocks, scampered about, and shook his head. "I don't know! I don't know!"

Yun Jiang did not ask more.

Three years passed.

Yun Jiang was again traveling in the east when he was passing through the wilderness of Song and he again happened on Hong Meng. Greatly delighted, he rushed to him and said, "Oh Celestial! Have you forgotten me? Have you forgotten me, sir?" He knelt and bowed repeatedly, touching his head to the ground, and asking Hong Meng to speak.

Hong Meng said: "I drift and I float without knowing what I seek. Wild and crazy, I don't know where I've been. I wander untethered, observing that nothing is wrong. What more do I need to know?"

"I also feel wild and crazy, and people from every clan follow me wherever I go. I can't stop them. Since they won't let me go, I want to hear a word from you."

"Disrupting the order of heaven undermines the nature of all living things. Mysterious heaven is prevented from

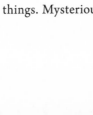

bringing all to completion. The herds are scattered. The birds cry all night long. Plants and trees wither. The insects suffer. Think! This is all due to the errors of people."

"Then what should I do?"

"Think! You're poisoning everything! Return to the way of the immortals!"

"I've found you with great difficulty. Please say more."

"Think! Nourish your heart! You must follow the way of nonaction. Then all things will be transformed by themselves. Go beyond your body, give up cleverness and brilliance, forget the relationship with all things that we consider normal. Make a great unity with all that is obscure as a watery and drizzly sea. Loosen your heart! Free your spirit! Be as nonexistent as if you had no soul!

"As multitudinous as the ten thousand things may be, each one returns to a root. Each one returns to its root without being conscious of it. They mix and merge in utter randomness, completely in their bodies without separation. If they became aware of this process, they would separate from it. But they don't ask any names. They do not try to see into themselves, and therefore, all things live within themselves."

"Oh Celestial. How I have gained from your virtue. You have revealed the mystery that I have been seeking all my life! Now I've gotten it!"

He bowed several times, touching his head to the ground. Then he stood up, said farewell, and went on his way.

Zhuangzi, "At Profundity" ⊤

101 | The Tao of the Early Kings

Today, some have kind hearts and benevolent knowledge, and yet the people do not receive any of their brilliance and no standards are set for the generations to follow. No one puts the Tao of the Early Kings into practice.

That's why there's this saying: "To follow excellence is not enough to govern. To merely set laws is not in itself advancement." The *Classic of Poetry* tells us: "Without transgression, without mistakes, follow the ancient statutes." No one who has respected the laws of the Early Kings has fallen into error.

Mengzi, "Li Lou I" ©

102 | What heart will you touch?

Deshan (Mount Virtue) Xuanjian (780/2–865) asked questions of his teacher, Longtan (Dragon Pool) Chongxin (760–840), until it was deep into the night. At last, Longtan said, "It's late. Son, why not retire?"

Deshan bowed, said goodnight, and lifted the screen to leave. Seeing only darkness, he turned and said, "It's black outside."

Longtan lit a candle inside a paper lantern and offered the handle to him. Deshan was about to take it when Longtan blew the candle out. At this, Deshan had a sudden recognition and he bowed respectfully.

Longtan said: "Son, what realization just appeared to you?"

"From today on, I will not doubt the tongue of the foremost old monk in the world."

The next day, Longtan rose before the assembly of the main hall and said, "Among you is a fellow with teeth like sword-trees and a mouth like a bloody basin. Strike him with a stick and he won't even turn his head. Someday, he alone will climb to the top of the highest peak and establish our noble Tao there."

Deshan brought all his notes to the front of the meditation hall, pointed a torch at them and said: "Even if you exhaust all the mysterious doctrines, it amounts to one thin hair in greatest emptiness. Even if you learn all the world's secrets, it amounts to no more than a drop in the great ocean."

Then he burned all his notes, bowed in farewell, and left his teacher.

WUMEN SAID: Prior to the time that Deshan crossed the mountain-pass, his heart was intense with anger, and his mouth spoke with bitterness. He went south, intending to stamp out all the doctrines of special transmission outside the sutras.

On the road to Lizhou, he asked an old woman to sell dimsum (literally, "touch the heart") to him. The old woman asked, "Your reverence, what literature do you have inside your cart?"

"Commentaries on the *Diamond Sutra*."

"I hear that the sutra says, 'The past heart cannot be gotten, the present heart cannot be gotten, and the future heart cannot be gotten.' Your reverence, what heart will you touch?"

Deshan had no answer for this question. But he did not remain completely bewildered by the old woman, and asked, "Do you know of a good teacher here?"

"Abbott Longtan is five miles from here."

Deshan went to Longtan, but he did not do well in the initial debates. What he said first did not match what he said afterward. Longtan seemed to have lost all sense of shame in his pity for the novice. Seeing that there was a spark in the student, he hurriedly poured muddy water to extinguish everything at once.

Cold earth is apparently one big laugh.

WUMEN'S VERSE:
Hearing the name is not like seeing the face.
Seeing the face is not like hearing the name.
Although he was able to save his nose,
but he could not help losing his eyes.

Wumenguan, Case 28 Ⓑ

103 | True friendship

Bo Ya excelled at playing the qin. Zhong Ziqi excelled at listening. As Bo Ya played, he thought of climbing a high mountain. Zhong Ziqi said: "Wonderful! This is as lofty as Mount Tai!" When Bo Ya thought of flowing waters, Zhong Ziqi said, "Splendid! Like the oceans! Like the rivers!" Bo Ya knew then that Ziqi and he were quite compatible.

Boya and he traveled north of Mount Tai when they were caught in a violent rainstorm. They were forced to take shelter beneath an overhanging cliff. Feeling downcast at heart, Bo Ya took up his qin and played to the copious rain. His music sounded as if the mountain itself was splitting apart. For every turn in the storm, Bo Ya played a response. Zhong Ziqi never flagged in his attention. When Bo Ya put his qin away, he sighed.

"Perfect, so perfect! You can hear my very intention. You can hear everything my heart imagines!"

Liezi, "Questions of Tang" Ⓣ

104 | Music is the root of action

Music comes from the heart,
the notes are the form of the music.
Lyrics, harmony, rhythm, composition
are the adornment of music:
the root of a noble one's actions.

Book of Rites, "Yue Ji" Ⓒ

105 | Tracing the source

Laozi said: In general, ten thousand things all go through a single opening. The root of one hundred matters all emerge from a single gate. Therefore, the sages track to a single standard, they do not deviate from what's original, and they do not change from what's constant. They permit themselves freedom and yet they follow a measure. They allow flexibility while they still follow what is constant.

When people are overjoyed or angry, it violates Tao. When they are overly sorrowful or grieved, they lose their virtue. When they think in terms of what pleases or repels them, they err in their hearts. When they indulge in their longings and desires, then their entanglements are born.

People in a great rage destroy their yin power. People who are overjoyed ruin their yang power. When their energy is thus weakened, they can't even speak. Their fright and terror drives them mad, and sadness and grief torch their hearts. Illness builds up. It is only when people can eliminate these problems that they can fuse themselves in a spiritual light.

Wenzi, "The Source of Tao" Ⓣ

"Men considered Lady Mao and imperial concubine Li the most beautiful of women," said Wang Ni, "but fish that saw those women dove away from them, birds soared from them into the sky, and elk scattered and fled. Yet, did any of those four—men, fish, birds, or elk—know what true womanly beauty was?

"As I view it, the principles of benevolence and righteousness similarly appear to be mere statements of right and wrong, thrown together, mixed up, and confused. I cannot begin to discuss them!"

"You don't even know the difference between good and bad," said Nie Que. "Would it follow that a realized person wouldn't be able to know either?"

"A realized person is divine! The great lakes could be boiling and a realized person would feel no heat. The Yellow and Han rivers could be frozen and a realized person wouldn't feel cold. Violent thunderbolts might cleave mountains, hurricanes might raise the oceans, and a realized person wouldn't be frightened. As such, they mount the clouds, ride on the sun and moon, and wander beyond the four seas. Matters of death and life won't alter them, so why would they bother with the principles of good and bad?"

Zhuangzi, "The Adjustment of Controversies" ⓣ

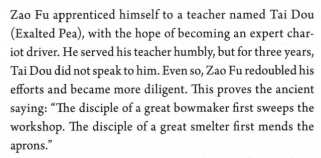

Zao Fu apprenticed himself to a teacher named Tai Dou (Exalted Pea), with the hope of becoming an expert chariot driver. He served his teacher humbly, but for three years, Tai Dou did not speak to him. Even so, Zao Fu redoubled his efforts and became more diligent. This proves the ancient saying: "The disciple of a great bowmaker first sweeps the workshop. The disciple of a great smelter first mends the aprons."

Finally, Tai Dou said: "You must first watch how I keep my concentration and do as I do. Only then can you drive a six-horse chariot."

"I will follow your command," said Zao Fu.

Tai Dou planted a number of posts into the ground. They were only a stride apart. He then stepped rapidly from post to post without stumbling or falling, and he never lost his concentration. Zao Fu set to practice. After three days, he was able to master the skill.

Then Tai Dou said: "You are clever. But can you become accomplished? This is how to drive a chariot:

"Before you move, set your feet, make your heart compliant, and drive forward. Keep the bit and reins uniform so that the horses will obey whether you want to go fast or slow. Keep them going straight, abreast, and even. Hold the reins lightly and calmly. Inside, keep your heart centered. Outside, blend your will and your horses. You can then make the horses go forward or backward, speed up or slow down, go in a circle, turn a curve, stay in the middle, or go straight.

Follow this Tao and you'll go far, with more than enough energy and strength. Then you'll truly realize this art.

"Skill is a matter of how you handle the reins. How you handle the reins depends on your hand. Your hands depend on your heart. Then you won't need to see with your eyes or use the whip. Your heart will be unencumbered. Your body will move efficiently. Even with six sets of reins, there will never be confusion. Twenty-four hooves will gallop without conflict. Circle! Advance! Retreat! You'll never lose your center. When you look behind the chariot, you won't see deep ruts, nor will your horses' hooves kick up much dirt. Whether you encounter steep mountains and gorges or expanses of streams and marshes, you'll see them as the same! That's all there is to my skill: you must learn it!"

Liezi, "Questions of Tang" Ⓣ

108 | Extending what humans can do

When the sages had seen as sharply as they could with their
    eyes,
they used the compass, square, level, and line
to make things square, round, level, and straight:
    nothing surpassed what they did.

When they had heard as closely as they could with their
    ears,
they used pitch-pipes to tune to the five tones:
    nothing surpassed what they did.

THE WAY OF HEART & BEAUTY

When they had thought as much as they could in their
      hearts,
they arranged government so that people did not suffer:
    their benevolence spread throughout the world.

Mengzi, "Li Lou I" ©

109 | Those who love others who are like themselves

All the ordinary people in the world love those who agree
with them and they scorn those who differ from them. That
they love those who are like them and that they scorn those
who are different is because, in their hearts, they want to be
above everyone else.

But of those who feel this way in their hearts, are they
truly better than anyone else? They actually rely on the expe-
riences of others, and in reality, their own abilities cannot
exceed the abilities of the multitude.

So when such people want to do something for their
nation, they resort to what three dynasties worth of kings
said was good—and they do not see the suffering that they
cause! They rely on luck. How many times has their reliance
on luck ruined a nation? Such people won't succeed even
once in ten thousand tries to preserve a country. In ten thousand tries, they will ruin a state every time.

How terrible that heads of state don't know this!

Zhuangzi, "At Profundity" ⑦

Heaven and earth may be great, but their changes are even. Although there are numerous beings, ruling them must be united. The masses may be multitudinous, but they need a leader. Leading must proceed from virtue and be perfected under heaven. Therefore, the profound ancients ruled the world by doing nothing and maintaining complete and divine virtue.

If we use Tao to view words, then the ruler of the world will be correct. If we use Tao to view distinctions, then the statesmen will be righteous and enlightened. If we use Tao to view abilities, then the officials will be orderly. If we use Tao to view all things widely, then all will be perfectly as they need to be.

Virtue pervades heaven and earth. Tao moves the ten thousand things. Officials rule by taking care of all endeavors. The capable gain their art through skill. Skill connects with taking care of matters. Taking care of matters connects with righteousness. Righteousness connects with virtue. Virtue connects with Tao. Tao connects with heaven.

Therefore it is said: "The ancients who care for the world had no desires but for the world to have enough. They did nothing and yet the ten thousand things were transformed. They were still as the abyss, and yet every clan was settled."

It is recorded: "With one channel, myriad endeavors are completed. No heart needs reward and the ghosts and spirits submit."

Zhuangzi, "Heaven and Earth" ⑦

111 | The way to deliberate in your heart

Now, a person who loses a needle may search all day and not find it. If they eventually find it, it won't be because their eyesight has improved. It will be because they've finally seen it.

You should deliberate this way in your heart too.

Xunzi, "Grand Digest" ©

112 | Without learning it can't be broken

Water is inside the pot,
  but without fire, it can't be warmed.
Grain is inside the ground,
  but without spring, it won't be grown.
Foolishness is inside the heart,
  but without learning it can't be broken.

Zibo Zhenke (1543–1603), *Recorded Sayings of Master Zibo* Ⓑ

113 | Keep your spirit in your heart

Laozi said: Heaven brings what's lofty. Earth brings what's substantial. The sun and moon shine. The array of stars glitter. Yin and yang are in harmony. There is no effort in any of this. They all properly follow Tao, and all things are natural.

Yin and yang and the four seasons do not birth the ten thousand things. Seasonal rain and dew don't nurture the grass and trees. It's spiritual brilliance and the harmonious interaction of yin and yang that birth the ten thousand things.

People of Tao store their essence within. They keep their spirits in their hearts. They are tranquil, aloof, peaceful, and cheerful. They are happy and calm inside their chests, broad as if they had no form, as quiet as being soundless. Government affairs will be seemingly without incident. The imperial court will seemingly have no crowds. There will be no suppressed scholars, no fleeing refugees, no forced labor, no unjust punishment.

All the world will look up to the image of an excellent leader. What is aberrant and vulgar in the country will be curtailed and excellent disclosure of information will be achieved. As if seeing one's home before one arrives, people will eagerly push forward with sincere hearts for the world and themselves.

Therefore, when rewarding the good and punishing brutality, make all your commands proper. If you're to act, do it with essential sincerity. Make your commands, but understand that you cannot act alone, and be sure to have sincerity. But be certain with Tao—or else people won't follow you and even sincerity won't be enough to cover you.

Wenzi, "Sincerity" Ⓣ

114 | Until I couldn't see anymore

Swallow after swallow circles in flight,
their sound comes from below and above.
She was returning to her home country
and I accompanied her far to the south.
I watched until I couldn't see her anymore,
and turmoil filled my heart.

Classic of Poetry, "Yan Yan" ©

115 | A heart that's always virtuous

The heart of one who can embrace and unite the world is high, superior, exalted, and precious. It is not arrogant toward others. It is brilliant with sagely wisdom. It slights no one. Its behavior is orderly, it communicates immediately, and it does not enter into disputes with others. It may be strong, resolute, brave, and daring, but it doesn't bully others. If it doesn't know, it asks. If it isn't able, it learns. Even if it is capable, it will still yield to others. And so its actions are always virtuous.

Xunzi, "Against the Twelve Masters" ©

116 | To see death and life together

The master said: "The Tao covers and carries the ten thousand things. How vast and great it is in scope! The noble one must give their heart to it!

Acting by doing nothing is called heaven. Doing nothing in speech is called virtue. Loving people and benefitting all things is called benevolence. Being different and yet at one with all is called greatness. Moving without trying to be distinguished is called broad. To have ten thousand differences is called abundance.

Therefore, to be virtuous is the standard. Complete virtue is called upstanding. Concord with Tao is called perfect. Not allowing anything to grind down your will is called wholeness. When the noble one understands these ten points, they keep all their endeavors sheathed, their hearts are large, and the movement of all things is fulfilled.

Such a person leaves gold buried in the hills; leaves pearls sunk in the gulf; does not try to profit from goods or wealth; does not go near riches and honors; does not rejoice in long life; does not mourn youth; does not glory in position; is not ashamed of being poor. Old age and youth are both unimportant to them, and position and poverty are not enough to mention. So the noble one does not try to seize all the gains in the world and claim them as their own. They do not try to rule over the world as if it's their own exclusive right.

Their position is enlightenment, for the ten thousand things to be in perfect unity, and for death and life to be seen together.

Zhuangzi, "Heaven and Earth"

117 | Not losing the root of one's heart

There are things that people like more than life, and things that they dislike more than death. Don't think that only good people are like that at heart. All people are. Virtue will be there as long as it is not lost.

Imagine a basket of rice and a bowl of soup. Having them means you live. Losing them means you die. But if someone gives them insultingly, even the lowliest porter wouldn't take them. Or if someone kicks and abuses people, then even a beggar wouldn't eat crumbs.

Yet when someone offers ten thousand gold pieces, even if it is improper and wrong, people will take it.

What could ten thousand gold pieces do for me? Should I take it to get beautiful mansions, a wife and concubines, and thereby be poor and needy no more?

But then, I pause and compare the first case where food was rejected—even though it could stave off death—to the second case—where a fortune could get me beautiful mansions, a wife, and concubines.

What could save me from death is rejected, but does that mean I should accept what will relieve all my poverty? Or should I reject that too?

That would be called losing the root of my heart.

Mengzi, "Gaozi I" ©

118 | However beautiful, weapons are ill omens

However beautiful, weapons
are tools of ill omen,
hateful to all beings.

Those who have Tao don't use them.
The prince usually values the left,
but values the right when using troops.
Armies are tools of ill omen
and they are not the tools of a prince.
They are used only as a last resort.

Calm and repose are better.
Force is not beautiful.
To call it beautiful
is to delight in killing people.
Those who kill people
can never carry out the will of the world.

Celebration proceeds on the left.
Mourning proceeds on the right.
The lieutenant stands on the left.
The high general stands on the right—
in the place of mourning.
He is the killer of multitudes.
Mourning, grief, and sobbing
surround him.
For he, the victor in war,
hands out funerals.

Daodejing, 31 Ⓣ

THE WAY OF **HEART & BEAUTY**

119 | The way to gain people is through their hearts

Jie and Zhou lost all under heaven
because they lost their people.
They lost their people
because they lost their hearts.

The Tao to gain all under heaven
is to first gain the people.
Then you gain all under heaven.

The Tao to gain people's hearts
is to gather what they want
and not force them to take what they don't want.

Then people will return to kindness
as water flows downward
and animals run to the wilds.

Mengzi, "Li Lou I" ©

THE
WAY
OF
H
E
A
R
T
&
B
E
A
U
T
Y

120 | Not worrying about what others think

Jian Wu questioned Sun Shu'ao: "Sir, you were chief minister three times and you did not glory in splendor. You were dismissed from that position three times, and you were not sad. I initially doubted you. Now I see how easily your breath passes your nostrils. You must use your heart uniquely—but how?"

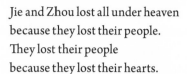

"How could I be better than other people?" said Sun Shu'ao. "When I was appointed, I could hardly refuse. When I was dismissed, I could hardly delay it. I regard gain and loss as having nothing to do with me, so why should I be sad? How can I be better than other people?

"Moreover, I did not know if the honor was in the position, or if the honor was in me. If it was in the position, it had nothing to do with me. If it was in me, it also had nothing to do with me. Since I had these uncertainties and since I was looking in all four directions, how did I have the time to worry whether people thought me valuable or worthless?"

Zhuangzi, "Tian Zifang" ⓣ

121 | Weeping for a veteran's heart

Where is the temple of the prime minister?
In Jin'guancheng, surrounded by lush cypress.
Green grass radiates spring colors on the steps,
yellow orioles part leaves to sing well in emptiness.

You served three times, so often troubled to plan the
      world—
an official through two dynasties with a veteran's heart.
But before complete victory, your body gave out,
and heroes' tears have drenched their coats ever since.

Du Fu (712–770), "Prime Minister of Shu" ⓛ

Beigongzi (Son of the Northern Palace) said to Ximenzi (Son of the West Gate): "Although we are of the same generation, people deem you more intelligent. Although we're from the same clan, people respect you more. Although we have the same looks, people love you more. Although we speak equally well, people flock to you. Although we are both upstanding people, people think you sincerer. Although we are both officials, only you've been promoted. Although we both own farms, your lands are more abundant. Although we both do business, you're the one who gets rich.

"My clothes are coarse and unbleached cotton. I eat the cheapest grades of millet and unpolished rice. I live in a ramshackle hut. When I go out, I have to walk. On the other hand, you dress in the most colorful brocades. You eat premium grains and the choicest meats. You live in a mansion with well-constructed beams. When you go out, your carriage is drawn by four horses. You have a splendid house but you never invite me there and that hurts me to my heart. In the king's court, you speak eloquently, but when you see me, you merely make small talk. I have asked to see you, but you won't stay in touch with me, and we don't travel together in the same circles or go to the same places. This has been going on for years. You really must think you're better than me!"

"I don't know if I'm better than you," said Ximenzi. "You've been inadequate in what you do, while I've been smart. Is that so hard to believe? Anyone would say so if they saw the two of us beside each other. Why, they could see it on your very face!"

Beigongzi did not know what else to do. Dejected, he started to walk back to his home.

On his way, he happened to encounter Mr. Dongguo (East City Walls), who said to him: "What has happened that you are now walking like this, with such shuffling steps and downcast looks?"

"I'm going back to my hut in embarrassment. If you want to know more, you can go ask Ximenzi."

Mr. Dongguo took Beigongzi to confront Ximenzi. "Did you humiliate Beigongzi and hurt his feelings?"

"Beigongzi found it strange that we are of the same generation, the same clan, of similar age, and of similar looks. He compared our speech, our conduct, his being overlooked and me promoted, him being poor and me being rich. I said that I didn't think that I was better than him, but I did note that he hadn't built much of a life for himself while I've been smart about building mine. It's obvious to anyone who compares us. That's why he looks so glum."

Mr. Dongguo said: "You talk only about success and failure. Don't mistake the difference between your own talent and virtue. I think of success and failure differently than you do. Beigongzi has great virtue, but he was destined to be poor. You were destined to be rich—but you have little virtue. You laud yourself as smart, but you are not wise. Beigongzi is poor, but it isn't because he's foolish or neglectful. It's because such things are determined by heaven and

not by people. You were fated to be rich and successful, and you feel proud. Beigongzi is deeply virtuous, but he feels ashamed. Neither of you recognizes the natural rationale of life."

"Stop, sir!" said Ximenzi. "I will never speak boastfully again!"

Beigongzi went home. Now he saw his rough, unbleached cotton clothes as being like luxurious furs. He saw his humble meal of beans and peas as the most-richly flavored foods. He felt that his hut was like the biggest and sturdiest mansion. He thought that a bamboo cart was like the most richly decorated imperial carriage. He was serene, and was no longer concerned with either success or failure.

Seeing this transformation, Mr. Dongguo remarked: "Beigongzi was like a man asleep. It only took one talk for him to wake! If only more people could become so enlightened!"

Liezi, "Effort and Destiny" ⑦

123 | Move softly yet with strength

Laozi said: Those who have Tao are mild in ambition but are strong in work. Their hearts are empty and yet they respond as is fitting. Those who are mild in ambition are as soft as down, peaceful and tranquil. They conceal themselves in nonacquisition, advance themselves but don't rely on their talent. They are calm and truly use nonaction and move without losing their timing. Therefore, the valuable is inevitably rooted in little-value; the high is inevitably based on the low.

Rely on the small to wrap the big. Establish the outer in the center. Move softly yet with strength. Then there is no power that you cannot overcome, no enemy that you cannot surmount. You must change to suit the times, then nothing will harm you.

Wenzi, "The Source of Tao" ⓣ

124 | To pacify the heart

Bodhidharma (fifth or sixth century BCE) sat facing a wall. The Second Patriarch (Dazu Huike; 487–593) cut off his arm and said, "Your student's heart is not yet at peace. I beg you, master: pacify my heart!"

"Bring your heart here and I will pacify it."

"I have searched for my heart but have not yet found it."

"Now your mind is indeed pacified!"

WUMEN SAID: "The broken-toothed old Hindu came so specially over thousands of miles of ocean. It could be said that he was raising waves where there was no wind. He finally got a disciple who was yet unqualified in six different ways. Why, Xie Sanlang did not even know four words."

Wumenguan, Case 33 Ⓑ

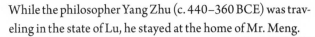

125 | Why aren't people content?

While the philosopher Yang Zhu (c. 440–360 BCE) was traveling in the state of Lu, he stayed at the home of Mr. Meng.

Mr. Meng asked: "Why aren't people content with themselves? Why do they still want fame?"

"They associate fame with wealth."

"But once they become wealthy, they still aren't content."

"That's because they then want to be prestigious and powerful."

"But even if they get that, they still aren't content."

"They become preoccupied with death."

"They can't overcome death, and they still aren't content."

"They nevertheless want to provide for their children and grandchildren."

"Can fame profit children and grandchildren?"

"Fame will bring bitter hardship to the body and it will scald the heart. Yet people still pursue fame as they try to bring brilliance to clan and family, to benefit their hometowns, and to promote all their associates. Of course they want to provide for their children and grandchildren too. But the pursuit of fame doesn't guarantee an honorable person; being an honorable person won't stave off poverty. Working for fame doesn't always guarantee sufficiency; sufficiency won't keep you from being worthless."

"That's reminiscent of Guan Zhong of the state of Qi. His emperor was lewd and licentious, and so was he. His emperor was extravagant and wasteful, and so was he. They joined wills in all that they said and did, and led the country by might rather than right. After his death, his clan declined.

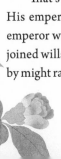

Now, let's take the case of Mr. Tian, also of the state of Qi. When his emperor was generous, he was reserved. When his emperor held back, he was giving. He was popular with the people because he always put the country first. Generations of his descendants have enjoyed good lives ever since. Thus, truly honorable means little fame. True wealth means to reject false fame."

"What has substance is without name. Fame is without substance. The pursuit of fame is false."

Liezi, "Yang Zhu" ⓣ

126 | A heart that embraces everything

The master said: Tao dwells in the depths. Its purity is limpid. It is beyond the reach of metal and stone. Such things will fall silent. Although metal and stone can make sounds, they can't sound those depths.

So who can decide all matters having to do with the ten thousand things? Only a person of royal virtue, someone who stays plain for all their life, who is humble and open in all endeavors. They stand, rooted and in touch with the source, with wisdom that is complete and spiritual. Therefore, their virtue is vast.

When their heart goes forth, it embraces everything that comes its way.

Zhuangzi, "Heaven and Earth" ⓣ

127 | The same things delight our hearts

All mouths relish the same flavors.
All ears relish the same sounds.
All eyes relish the same beauty.
When it comes to the heart,
can it be the only case
that is not the same?

If you ask me what's right:
    The sages already knew
    that my heart would have the same nature as all others.
    Therefore, their reason and righteousness delight my
        heart,
    just as food delights my mouth.

Mengzi, "Gaozi I" ©

128 | A heart offering

A face without anger
    is an offering.
A mouth without anger inside
    is wonderful and sweet.
A heart without anger
    is a precious jewel—
unceasing, indestructible,
    it is constant and true.

Anonymous, ancient Buddhist verse Ⓑ

113

Yang Zhu said: "People think it's a great achievement to live for one hundred years. But not one in a thousand accomplishes that.

"Take one person as an example. Add the years of being a babe in arms to the infirmity of the twilight years, and it takes up half their lifespan. Sleeping at night and waking activities during the day take up half of what's left. From that, let's subtract pain, illness, hardship, suffering, loss, grief, and fear. That takes up at least half of what's left again. I count about ten years left. During that period, how many times can we forget our worries?

"Why, then, do we live? What is happiness? Merely to pursue beauty and abundance? For beauty and sex? But beauty and abundance are not always enough. Music and sex can't be enjoyed without cares.

"Moreover, we're restricted by punishments and driven by rewards, drawn by fame and obstructed by laws. We busily hurry to compete for a short period of empty reputation, and we want a surplus of glory after we die. Utterly alone, we submit to what our eyes see and our ears hear, and we begrudge what is right and wrong for our bodies and minds. Thus, we lose the full joy of our best years, and we cannot indulge ourselves for even a moment. Are we any different than a convict in chains?

"The ancients knew that life comes briefly. They knew that death goes quickly. Therefore, they followed their own hearts in all that they did. They never violated the good of

THE WAY OF HEART & BEAUTY

what was natural. They didn't avoid whatever they found pleasurable, and they did not follow common views. They followed their own inner natures, even when they were abroad, and they never went against what was good for all living creatures. They did not strive for a reputation that would last beyond their deaths and they did not not try to conform to social rules. Name, fame, position; whether the years of life are many or few—these were unimportant considerations to them."

Liezi, "Yang Zhu" ⓣ

130 | The scheming heart

Laozi said: Cunning and scheming hidden within a heart adulterates one's purity. Such a heart appears genial but lacks any true colors, is dull-witted and without any edge. It stumbles and pitches forward. Looking, it cannot see. Standing, it's as if over a dry well. Plowing, it's like working a barren field. It does not wrap itself in giving. It does not seek virtue. It does not reach the level of either high or low. It does not find form in either long or short. In manners and regularity, it only follows the vulgar. Wanting to only do business easily, it wants sympathy, the fake, and to confuse the world. It drives on by charming people.

The sage does not engage in such vulgarity.

Wenzi, "The Source of Tao" ⓣ

So it's said: "When the world reaches softness, then the world instantly reaches hardness. There is no space to enter between them."

The formless is the great ancestor to all things. The soundless is the great ancestor of every category of things. The True Persons pass from a spiritual place and they help bring change to people by keeping profound virtue in their heart. Once there's change, it runs as quickly as a spirit.

That is why the inexplicable Tao is great indeed. Well before there's any sign, it has already mandated the season, shifted the wind, changed customs, and certainly moves the heart too.

The ten thousand things generate continuously, but they only have one root. The one hundred affairs issue forth continuously, but they are protected within their gate. Therefore, what can seemingly be exhausted is not exhausted. What is seemingly limited has no limits. Things shine forth but they are not confused. Sounds occur as they should even without being known.

Wenzi, "The Source of Tao" ⓣ

Confucius went to Lao Dan to speak of benevolence and righteousness. Lao Dan said:

"If you winnow chaff and the dust gets in your eyes, then even the four cardinal points of heaven and earth will be altered for you. If mosquitoes and gadflies bite your skin, then you won't be able to sleep for an entire night. In the same way, this dull talk of benevolence and righteousness irritates hearts and creates much confusion.

"I would rather that everyone always be simple. I would have them be free as the wind in all their movements, and establish themselves in total virtue! Why must you repeatedly be like a great hero who beats a drum as he tries to find his lost son?

"The snow-goose doesn't bathe itself each day to stay white. The crow doesn't paint itself each day to stay black. They are simply white and black. They don't need your clever words. They don't need to be admired as being famous and celebrated. They don't need to try to be greater than what they are.

"When the springs dry up, the fish huddle together in the dirt. They gasp on each other, trying to keep themselves moist with their foam. It would be better if they didn't need to worry about one another and instead swam in the rivers and lakes."

Zhuangzi, "The Movement of Heaven" ⓣ

THE WAY OF HEART & BEAUTY

117

133 | How standards are overrun

In ancient times, what was called being a scholar meant a person with abundant virtue, someone capable of great calm, who cultivated correctness, who understood the commands of life, and who stood straight for right.

Nowadays, what is called being a scholar means a person with no abilities who insists that they are capable; who has no knowledge while declaring that they are knowledgeable; who seeks limitless gain for their own heart while pretending to be dispassionate; who advances the false, dangerous, and obscene while pretending to be upright, lofty, trustworthy, and honest. They make the abnormal their normal, and indulge themselves while slandering others.

Xunzi, "Against the Twelve Masters" ©

134 | Is this very heart Buddha?

Damei Fachang (?–839) asked his teacher, Mazu Daoyi (709–788): "What is Buddha?"

Mazu (Ancestor Ma) said: "This very heart is Buddha."

WUMEN SAID: "If you can directly appreciate this, then you wear Buddha's robes, eat Buddha's food, speak Buddha's words, do the Buddha's deeds—that is, you are Buddha.

"Even so, Damei led several people into taking the mark on the balance beam for the weight itself. How could he understand that to utter the word 'Buddha' should call for

three days of rinsing out one's mouth? If anyone should hear this phrase, 'This very heart is Buddha,' they should cover their ears and run away."

WUMEN'S VERSE:
Blue sky, bright day.
By all means, avoid more searching.
If you ask how even more,
is to claim injustice while holding stolen goods.

Wumenguan, Case 30 Ⓑ ◎

135 | Would you give a hair to save the world?

Yang Zhu said: "Bocheng Zigao wouldn't give a hair to benefit others, and he became a hermit. Yu the Great never used his body for his own self-interest, and he made himself into a withered cripple. The ancients said that if no one gave a hair to try to help the world, nothing would be gained. If no one offered their body to help the world, then nothing would be lost. No one wants to give a hair. No one wants to help the world. And yet the world is orderly."

A man named Qinzi said to Yang Zhu: "If giving a strand of your hair would help the world, would you do it?"

"The world wouldn't be helped by a strand of my hair."

"But if it did, would you?"

Yang Zhu did not answer.

Sometime later, Qinzi met Meng Sunyang and recounted the dialogue. Meng said: "You don't understand the meaning in Yang Zhu's heart. Let me ask you this: Would you cut off a piece of your flesh for ten thousand pieces of gold?"

"I would."

"But would you cut off a limb to gain a country?"

Qinzi was silent.

"A strand of hair is minor compared to a piece of flesh. A piece of flesh is minor compared to a limb. However, the accumulation of hair completes one's flesh, the accumulation of flesh completes a limb. One hair contributes to one body, ten thousand parts contribute to one being. Where do you draw the line of what's insignificant?"

"I have no answer. If I were to ask Lao Dan or Guan Yin, they would probably agree with you. But if I were to ask Yu the Great or Mozi, they would agree with me."

Liezi, "Yang Zhu" ⊕

136 | Knowing how to sort things out

Here's a man whose finger is bent and can't be straightened.

It isn't diseased or painful, and it doesn't interfere with his daily business. But if he heard that there was someone who could make it straight, he wouldn't think it too far to go from Qin to the next country of Chu—all because his finger was not as good as those of other people.

When a man's finger isn't as good anyone else's he knows how to be upset. But if his heart isn't as good as those of other people, he does not know to feel upset.

This is called not knowing how to sort things out.

Mengzi, "Gaozi I" ©

137 | Not Buddha, not Tao

Nanquan said: "The heart is not Buddha. Wisdom is not Tao."

WUMEN SAID: "It could be said that Nanquan was old and shameless. Just by opening his stinking mouth, he lets out the family scandal. Even so, few know of his kindness."

WUMEN'S VERSE:
The sky clears, the sun comes out.
Rain falls and soaks the earth.
As much as he likes, he says it all,
but I'm afraid he isn't fully believed.

Wumenguan, Case 34 ⓑ

Laozi said: Heaven manifests the sun and the moon; arranges the stars and planets; extends the four seasons; and moves yin and yang.

It is the sun's power and the night's rest; it dries with the wind and moistens with the rain and dew. In birthing all things, it nurtures and invisibly preserves the ten thousand things. In destroying all things, it terminates and invisibly brings death to the ten thousand things. This is called spiritual and sacred.

This is why the sages take heaven as their guiding image. They raise happiness; although no one sees them, blessings arise. They relieve disasters; although no one sees them, disasters are relieved.

Examine insufficiency. Investigate the false. Plan each day for what is meager. Plan each year so you'll have surplus. Stillness is soundless and one word moves the whole world because heaven's heart motivates all change.

Therefore, sincerity is inside all form. Energy moves in heaven, the stars appear to our sight. Yellow dragons descend. Phoenixes arrive. Fountains of sweet wine burst forth. Auspicious crops sprout. The rivers will not flood. The oceans will have no tidal waves.

But if we disobey heaven and brutalize living things, the sun and moon will be eclipsed; the cardinal stars fail to revolve; the order of the four seasons will be disrupted; daytime will brighten until the nights glow; mountains will collapse and rivers will dry up; the winter will have thunderstorms and summers will freeze.

Those who follow heaven are in communication with each other, and so they prevent the destruction of their country. Heaven's signs change. Where the world was confused, rainbows appear.

The ten thousand things are interconnected. If essence and energy were both to decline, it would be a matter of the divine light. We would not know what to do. We would not know what power caused it to happen.

That is why the great people follow heaven and earth's combined virtue. They follow the sun and moon's combined brilliance. They follow the ghosts and gods' combined spirituality. They follow the four season's truth. They put heaven's heart into their own chests. They embrace the energy of the earth. They take all that flows toward them and store that up as harmony. They walk the four seas without leaving their halls. They study transformation and change social customs so people improve. This is the enabling of spiritual change.

Wenzi, "Sincerity" ⓣ

139 | Three precepts

If your speech will not benefit others,

do not speak.

If your heart's thoughts will not benefit others,

do not think.

If your footsteps will not benefit others,

do not walk.

Gaofeng Yuanmiao (1238–1295), *Records of Chan Master Gaofeng Yuanmiao* ©

123

140 | Traveling to the beginning of all things

Confucius went to visit Lao Dan. When he arrived, Lao Dan had just finished bathing, and was letting his long hair dry. He was so motionless that he didn't even seem alive. Confucius relaxed and waited.

When the time came to talk, he said: "Was I confused? Was that really you? You looked like a hollowed-out stump, having abandoned all things, and separated from all people to be in solitude."

"My heart traveled to the beginning of all things," said Lao Dan.

"Can you describe that?"

"My heart finds it difficult and I'm not sure that I know how. I open my mouth, but I can't find the words. But I'll try to tell you.

"I reached yin, and all was severe and grave. I reached yang, and all was radiant and bright. The severe and grave come from heaven. The radiant and bright come from the earth. The two mixed and completed themselves in harmony and all things were produced. If someone regulates this, no one has seen their form. Vanishing and resting, filling and emptying, one dark, one light, the changes of the sun and the alterations of the moon—these occur daily, but no one has seen anyone working.

"Life is sprouting. Death is returning. Beginning and ending follow one another without cease. Either way, no one does this as if there's some grand ancestor!"

Zhuangzi, "Tian Zifang" ⊤

141 | Tao without method

Laozi said: The people of Tao keep their inner natures intact and protect their genuineness. They don't let themselves be injured. They meet all encounters directly and forcefully resolve difficulties.

When their essence penetrates to heaven, seemingly exceeding their purpose, what action would be unsuccessful?

Then death and life are of the same realm, there will be no threat of maltreatment, and every situation will be treated as if it's for the sake of heaven and earth. They carry the ten thousand things, return to nature, and cherish the achievement of harmony—that's nothing more than being undying.

Sincerity within them goes outwardly into others' hearts. This is the Tao that is beyond teaching. When the sages are on high, they embrace the Tao and they do not speak; their grace extends to all people, and yet they give no verbal instructions. Their influence is great indeed! By contrast, when ruler and officials are of crafty hearts, their multiple deeds of cunning are noticed by heaven. Divine energy will respond to the very smallest level.

This is what is meant by, "ruling without words," and the "Tao without method."

Wenzi, "Sincerity" ⑦

142 | The importance of attention

It is not surprising when a king is unwise. For example, take the easiest thing to grow in this world. Give it one day of warmth, followed by ten days of cold. It won't grow. I might see the king to give advice, but afterward others will descend like the cold. I might have brought about some buds, but what good is it?

Now, *weiqi* (similar to the Japanese game of Go) is a minor art, and yet unless you give it your whole heart and will, you will not be able to play well.

Yi Qiu was the best weiqi player in the entire kingdom. Suppose he was teaching two people how to play: one person uses their whole heart and will to follow everything that they hear. The other seems to be listening, but then their heart sees a flock of wild swans drawing near and wants to use a bow and arrows to shoot them. Both are learning beside each other, but they aren't the same kind of student.

Is it because their intelligence is unequal? That is not so.

Mengzi, "Gaozi I" ©

143 | My heart profits from being small

A man asked Sun Shuao: "People have three faults. Do you know what they are?"

"What do you mean?" Sun asked.

"High rank makes people jealous. Greatness as an official invites the enmity of lords. Substantial wealth brings resentment from far away."

"In rank, I give profit to those above me. In purpose, I give profit to those below me. In official life, I give profit to those who are greater.

"My heart profits from being small. My wealth profits from being thick. My charity profits from being broad. This is how I avoid those three faults. What do you think?"

Liezi, "Explaining Coincidences" Ⓣ

144 | The best fit

Worker Chui could make things rounder than if he had used a compass. His fingers had the same power as that which transforms all things and he didn't have to rely on anything conscious from his heart. His soul was one and he had no restrictions.

A shoe should fit without the foot being aware of it. A belt should fit without the waist being aware of it. Wisdom should forget what is or isn't. Being aware of either inner transformations or outer attractions fit the heart best. That also fits how we should meet every endeavor.

To have the sense of fitting from the start and never to experience what does not fit is to have the fitting that can forget fitting.

Zhuangzi, "Attaining Life" Ⓣ

127

145 | All the world knows beauty as beautiful

All the world knows beauty as beautiful—
    and so they know ugliness too.
Everyone knows goodness as good—
    and so they know bad too.

So nothing and things are born together,
difficulty and ease complete one another,
long and short make one another,
high and low come from one another,
pitch and tone harmonize with each other,
before and after follow one another.

Accordingly, the wise carry out all matters
without trying for their own results.
They teach without using words,
let all things flourish without instruction
and let them grow without anyone owning them.

All will grow without anyone saying so,
and all results happen without anyone's orders.
All work is done without anyone doing it:
this will never go away.

Daodejing, 2 Ⓣ

146 | Like a mantis waving at a cart

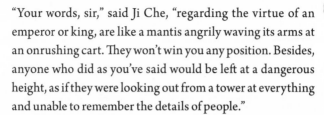

"Your words, sir," said Ji Che, "regarding the virtue of an emperor or king, are like a mantis angrily waving its arms at an onrushing cart. They won't win you any position. Besides, anyone who did as you've said would be left at a dangerous height, as if they were looking out from a tower at everything and unable to remember the details of people."

Jiang Lu'mian was startled, and murmured, "I'm taken aback by what you've said. I'd like to hear how you think a ruler should influence people."

"When a great sage administers the world, they cleanse the people's hearts. They send out envoys to lead the alteration of all the social customs. They eliminate all treacherous hearts, and fix everyone on a single purpose. They would feel that all that they did came from their own natures without knowing why they wanted to be that way. If this was so, then the teachings to the people of the elders Yao and Shun would become junior and fall into obscurity. All would join in virtue and remain of the heart."

Zhuangzi, "Heaven and Earth" Ⓣ

THE
WAY
OF
H
E
A
R
T
&
B
E
A
U
T
Y

Confucius was in discussion with Lao Dan and said, "Today is peaceful and leisurely. May I ask about realizing Tao?"

Lao Dan said: "You must fast and keep a vigil. Relax and clear your heart. Let your essence and spirit be pure as snow. Be severe and strong, yet wise. Tao is a deep subject and difficult to describe. I can only give you a rough outline.

"The light and luminous was born from the dark and obscure. The varied was born from the formless. Essence and spirit were born from Tao, and the root of all form was born from essence. After this, the ten thousand things were born together.

"Thus, creatures with the nine apertures were born from the womb, and those with eight apertures were born from eggs. But their coming leaves no trace, and their going leaves no residue. They need no gate and no house because they can come from any of the four directions like the kingliest king. Coming into the world like this, their four limbs are strong.

"Thoughtful, concerned, honest, and intelligent; their ears and eyes brilliant and bright; they can use their hearts without effort. They need no convention in responding to things as they should.

"If heaven had not achieved this, it would not be high. If earth had not achieved this, it would not be broad. If the sun and moon had not achieved this, they would not move. If the ten thousand things had not achieved this, they would not flourish. That's what Tao gives them!"

Zhuangzi, "Knowledge While Roaming in the North" ⊤

Penetrate the will's impulse to be quick.
Undo the bindings of your heart.
Get rid of the impediments to virtue.
Go beyond obstructions to Tao.

Riches and honor; distinction and rigor; fame and profit—
    these six stimulate the will's impulse to be quick.
Appearance, movement, lust, control, energy, intention—
    these six bind the heart.
Hatred and longing; joy and rage; sorrow and happiness—
    these six impede virtue.
Distance and approach; conquest and opposition;
        knowledge and ability—
    these six obstruct Tao.
When these four conditions with their six factors
    no longer toss inside your chest, then all will be well.

To be well means to be quiet.
To be quiet means to be bright.
To be bright means to be empty.
To be empty means the nonaction that achieves
    by not achieving.

Zhuangzi, "Gengsang Chu" Ⓣ

THE WAY OF HEART & BEAUTY

131

149 | One suffers hardship to become great

When heaven wants to confer a great duty on a person,
it will first subject their heart to hardship,
their muscles and bones to labor,
and their body to hunger.
Their efforts will be confounded,
so that their heart is moved,
their nature become enduring,
and their shortcomings augmented.

People always err,
but they can improve.
Their hearts will be besieged,
they will ponder and worry,
but they will rise afterward.
They will flush with color,
their words will pour forth,
and they will come to a new stature.

Mengzi, "Gaozi II" ©

150 | Your toiling heart

Don't farm huge fields—
    the weeds will run rampant.
Don't think of those far away—
    your belabored heart will grieve.

Classic of Poetry, "Fu Tian" Ⓛ

151 | Pity those who pity others

Nanbo Ziqi was seated behind a small table, sighing as his head was raised heavenward. His student, Yan Chengzi, came in, saw him, and said: "Master, you are extraordinary. How can you make your body like a decaying skeleton and your heart like dead ashes?"

"When I once lived in a mountain cave, Tian He came to visit me. All the people of Qi congratulated him three times for having found me.

"I must first have shown myself for him to know me. I must have been selling something for him to come to buy. If I didn't exist, who would have known me? If I had not been selling, how would he have come to buy? Alas!

"I pity those who lose themselves. I also pity those who pity others. I also pity others who pity others who pity others. They are left behind, and are left far away."

Zhuangzi, "Xu Wugui" Ⓣ

152 | Stopping bad doctrines

It is said: "A ball rolling in a bowl will stop soon. Rolling talk will stop when it meets wisdom." That's why bad doctrines from different schools damage discourse. When what *is* or *isn't* is in doubt, then measure by matters far, examine by comparing to what is near, and consider it all with a balanced heart. Stop wayward talk, and bad doctrines will die.

Xunzi, "Grand Digest" Ⓒ

153 | The sages conceal themselves

Confucius went to the state of Chu and found lodging with a congee-seller on Ant Hill. A man, his wife, his concubines, and his servants were in a house next door. Confucius's student, Zilu, asked, "What are those people doing there?"

"That is a disciple of the sages," Confucius said. "He is concealing himself among the people and he secrets himself along the paths between the fields. His voice is finished. His will has diminished. Even if he speaks out loud, his heart has no taste for the words. He is no longer given to his era, and his heart doesn't care to scramble for crumbs. He'd rather sink into the ground. Could he be Shi'nan Yiliao?"

Zilu wanted to call on the man, but Confucius said, "Stop! He knows that I understand him. He knows that I've traveled to Chu and thinks that I will ask the king of Chu to summon him to court. He thinks I am a flatterer, and because of that, he thinks it would be a disgrace to listen to me, much less see me. Why do you think he would stay there?"

Zilu rushed over to the other house, but found every room empty.

Zhuangzi, "Zeyang" Ⓣ

134

Some raise up the poor and relieve the anxious, while others want fame and to raise their profits.

Get rid of evil—namely the drive for achievement and success—and there would be no calamity in this world, all would be peaceful from top to bottom without needing sages to dispense virtue, and all would be accomplished without worthy people having to establish it. Therefore, the realized person treats others by enclosing them in virtue and embracing them in Tao. They advance sincerity, and bestow boundless wisdom. They put speech aside and use no words, and no one in this world ever knows the value of such wordlessness.

Therefore: "The Tao that is spoken is not the constant Tao. The name that is named is not the constant name." That is written on the bamboo tablets. It is engraved on metal and stone. It has been handed down to refine coarse people.

The Three Sovereigns, Five Emperors, and Three Kings were each unique in what they did, but the wishes in their heart were the same. They walked different roads, but their accomplishments were the same. Before the world learned, we did not know the importance of committing ourselves— tracking, kneeling, sitting—to complete every task with the same solid and single virtue.

No matter how learned we are, we must seek this often if we are to be saved from confusion.

Wenzi, "Sincerity" Ⓣ

THE WAY OF HEART & BEAUTY

155 | All people have value

In their hearts, all people want to be valued, and all people are naturally valuable.

However, we don't usually think in that way. We think that value comes from others, but that is not real value: what an arbiter might laud as valuable, that arbiter can later label worthless.

The *Classic of Poetry* states: "As if drunk on wine, you're already filled with virtue."

By saying "filled," it means that you're already filled with kindness and righteousness.

Therefore, forget the hankering to taste rich meats and fine grains; or to have high titles and fame; or to have a wide reputation conferred on you. Leave any longing for richly embroidered robes.

Mengzi, "Gaozi II" ©

156 | What the world honors

This world honors
    wealth, status, long life, and joy.
It delights in
    a healthy body, rich flavor, beautiful fashion, good sex,
        and exciting music.
It disdains
    poverty, low status, short life, and misery.

It considers bitterness to be:
>   a mouth that tastes no rich flavors,
>   a body that wears no beautiful fashions,
>   eyes that see no good sexual partners,
>   ears that hear no exciting music.
> If people do not get these
>   they feel fearful and sad.

They do this all for their bodies.
>   How sad!

Zhuangzi, "Perfect Enjoyment" Ⓣ

157 | Reconciliation

Blowing steadily, the valley wind
brings clouds, then rain.
Let us strive to be of one heart:
it's not right to hold onto anger.
We pick turnips and gather melons
but we don't take their lower parts.
Don't betray our heartfelt murmurs:
I'll be with you until we die together.

Classic of Poetry, "Gu Feng" Ⓛ

And so, if you accumulate soil, you can form a mountain. If you accumulate water, you can form a sea. If you accumulate dawns and dusk, you can call it a year. If you reach high, you call that the sky. If you reach low, you say it's the earth. The six directions in the world are called the extremes. If all the ordinary people in the world of every name were to accumulate goodness whole and complete, we could call them all sages.

They must seek it to attain it. They must work to achieve it. Only with accumulation can there be loftiness thereafter. They must do their utmost, and only then will sagacity follow. Therefore, sages are people of accumulation.

Those who accumulate experience in weeding and plowing become farmers. Those who accumulate experience in chopping and carving become craftspersons. Those who accumulate experience in selling and marketing become merchants. Those who accumulate experience in ritual and righteousness become noble ones.

The children of craftspeople continue their fathers' work. Similarly, the people of a country readily follow the national dress. Those who live in Chu follow the style of Chu; those who live in Yue follow the style of Yue. Those who live in Xia follow the style of Xia. This is not a matter of any heaven-given nature, but because of accumulation and distribution.

So if people know how to be attentive and focused, if they avoid blunders and are careful in their habits, they will have

a great and wide accumulation. Then they will become noble ones.

If they indulge in their inborn natures and do not question or learn enough, they then will become inferior people. The noble ones have everlasting tranquility and glory. The inferior ones have everlasting danger and disgrace. Everyone wants tranquility and glory, but only the noble one can have such goodness, while the inferior one is on the edge of harm every day.

The *Classic of Poetry* states:

Safeguard the virtuous people.
Don't seek the unenlightened—
only the ones with patient hearts.
Look back on this repeatedly:
greedy and disorderly people
poison peace with bitterness.

Xunzi, "Achievements of the Ru" ©

159 | Don't let your heart be dark

Do not let your own heart be dark.
Do not point out the faults of others.
Be prudent in exchanges and don't get upset.
Work patiently and have good discussions.

Hanshan Deqing (1546–1623), "Vital Discussions" ⓑ

As if using the hook, line, compass, and square to make our-selves correct, we hack away at our personalities. As if using cords, fasteners, glue, and varnish to build ourselves, we dis-tort our natural virtue. Some people use the rites and music to bend and shape, and they roar about benevolence and righteousness to subdue the hearts of everyone in the world. This fails to understand what is inherently natural.

This world has an inherent nature. In this true nature, what is bent needs no hook. What is straight needs no line. What is round needs no compass. What has corners needs no square. What is attached needs neither glue nor varnish. What holds together needs neither cords nor bands.

Therefore, everything in the world can grow naturally by itself. Those things might not know how they were born. They just know what they have, and they don't care about what they don't have. It was so in ancient times, and it's so now, and this will go on forever.

Why, then, use the concepts of benevolence and righ-teousness to try to hold personalities together as if endlessly joining with glue, varnish, cords, and bands, hindering a per-son from roaming in the space of the vital Tao? It misleads the entire world!

And where there is great deceit, then human nature itself is altered!

Zhuangzi, "Webbed Toes" ⓣ

161 | The vital essence of the heart

Laozi said: The vital essence of the heart can be made spiritual, but not by verbal methods.

The sages do not leave their mats, and yet they can rectify the world because they use feelings over spoken words. That's because trying to get agreement through words is not reliable—trust must come before words—and agreeing to the commands to action must have sincere orders.

When the sages are in command, the people are mysteriously transformed because feelings have been put first. Then all progresses upward rather than downward. It makes all the difference that the sages command through feeling.

A three-month-old infant does not yet know of benefit and harm, yet the mercy of motherly love can heal serious illness. That's because of feeling too.

Therefore, to use words to try to achieve transformation is negligible. Not to use words to try to achieve transformation is great. Trust should be the noble one's word. Loyalty should be the noble one's intention. Loyalty and trust must be on the inside before anyone's heart can be moved on the outside. This is the way that the virtuous sages bring about change.

Wenzi, "Sincerity" ⊤

Confucius was conversing with Lao Dan and said, "Today is peaceful and leisurely. May I ask about realizing Tao?"

Lao Dan said: "You must fast and keep a vigil. Relax and clear your heart. Let your essence and spirit be pure as snow. Be severe and strong, yet wise. Tao is a deep subject and difficult to describe. I can only give you a rough outline.

"The light and luminous was born from the dark and obscure. The varied was born from the formless. Essence and spirit were born from Tao, and the root of all form was born from essence. After this, the ten thousand things were born together.

"Thus, creatures with the nine apertures were born from the womb, and those with eight apertures were born from eggs. But their coming leaves no trace, and their going leaves no residue. They need no gate and no house because they can come from any of the four directions like the kingliest king. Coming into the world like this, their four limbs are strong.

"Thoughtful, concerned, honest, and intelligent; their ears and eyes brilliant and bright; they can use their hearts without effort. They need no convention in responding to things as they should.

"If heaven had not achieved this, it would not be high. If earth had not achieved this, it would not be broad. If the sun and moon had not achieved this, they would not move. If the ten thousand things had not achieved this, they would not flourish. That's what Tao gives them!"

Zhuangzi, "Knowledge While Roaming in the North" ①

THE
WAY
OF

H
E
A
R
T

&

B
E
A
U
T
Y

163 | The nirvana heart

From the distant past until now, Buddha's teachings reveal the workings of cause-and-effect. Each case has been given completely in their original form. The author has taken the lid off his brain and exposed his eyes so that others will straightaway bear down themselves and not follow others. If you are an open and superior person of cultivation, you will know at the slightest mention. There is no gate that can be entered. There are no stairs to climb. Squaring your shoulders, you go through the mountain pass without having to ask the guard.

Remember what Xuansha Shibei (835–908) said: "No gate is the gate to be freed of worldly worries. No meaning is the meaning to a person of Tao."

Baiyun Shouduan (1025–1072) said: "Obviously you know, but why can't you pass through?"

But all this talk amounts to red dust smeared on a cow. If you go through the no-gate mountain pass, then you make a fool of No-Gate. If you do not go through the no-gate mountain pass, then you are only failing yourself.

It is easy to dawn on the nirvana heart, but hard to understand the wisdom of distinction. When you have reached the understanding of the wisdom of distinction, then your own home and country will be at peace.

Wumenguan, Postscript Ⓑ

The border-warden of Changwu said to Zilao: "In governing, a ruler must not be like someone who fails to clear the rock and underbrush from the land. In administering the people, a ruler must not be like someone who carelessly pulls up shoots. Before, when I was plowing my field for grain, I did not clear the rock and underbrush well, and the result was telling. In weeding, I carelessly pulled up shoots too, and the result was telling. In subsequent years, I changed completely. I plowed deeply and raked well. The grain thrived. We had more than we could eat for the entire year."

When Zhuangzi heard this, he said, "Nowadays, when people care for their bodies and manage their hearts, most are like this border-warden's first actions. They obscure their own divinity, separate from their inner natures, extinguish their emotions, and destroy their spirits just to be like everyone else.

"Thus, when it comes to their own natures, they leave the rock and underbrush. Desire and the worst of their faults are taken as their nature. Sedges, weeds, and rushes begin to sprout within us, and gradually uproot our natures. We are defeated, little by little. If we don't choose to pluck them out, we become scabbed and ulcerated, suffering from fever and oozing greasiness indeed."

Zhuangzi, "Zeyang" ⏀

165 | True words are not beautiful

True words are not beautiful.
Beautiful words are not true.

Excellence does not deceive.
Deceit is not excellent.

Wisdom isn't broad.
Breadth is not wise.

Sages don't accumulate.
When they do for others they do more for themselves.
When they give to others they give more to themselves.

Heaven's Tao is sharp but not harmful.
Sages' Tao serves and never strives.

Daodejing, 81 ⓣ

THE WAY OF HEART & BEAUTY

166 | The impulse to worship

Out of all the rules of Tao, none is more urgent than ritual.
Ritual has five aspects, and the most important is worship.
Worship is not external.
It comes from inside.
It is born in the heart.
When our hearts are moved,
we want to make offerings through worship.
That is why only the sincere can worship well.

Book of Rites, "Ji Tong" ©

145

167 | The foolish heart

End learning and there will be no grief.
Between "ah" and "hem,"
how much difference is between the two?
Between good and bad,
how do we choose between them?
What all people fear
has to be feared.
And yet we still don't know what to do!

Everyone looks satisfied and pleased,
as if enjoying a great banquet,
or as if climbing a terrace in spring.
I am alone, not knowing what's ahead,
like an infant who isn't yet grown,
or like one worn and bleak
with no home to return to.

Everyone has more than enough—
I alone seem to have lost it all.
Mine is a foolish man's heart!

I'm in chaos and confusion!
I'm the only one in darkness!
Normal people are clever and sure
while I am all out to sea,
buffeted by ceaseless winds!

Everyone has their places.
I alone am stubborn and glum.

I alone am different from other people:
I value succor from Mother.

Daodejing, 20 ⓣ

168 | What desire cannot do

Laozi said: Sages cannot overcome their hearts. Ordinary people cannot overcome their desires. The noble one walks with justice. The petty person walks in wickedness. Inside, one should have an easy nature. Outside one should accord with righteousness. Follow the patterns, but keep moving; don't become attached to things and be upright.

Reject the pursuit of exciting flavor; excess in noise and color; reaction to pleasure and anger. Don't chase these, because there will only be suffering after. This is wickedness.

Wickedness and righteousness injure each other. Desire and one's inner nature harm each other. One side cannot stand with the other: when one rises, the other falls. Therefore, the sage abandons desires in order to follow their inner nature.

The eyes like color. The ears like sound. The nose likes fragrance. The mouth likes flavor. Together, we must say that they are never separate from gain and loss—and lust too. The ears, eyes, nose, and mouth don't know what to want. It's the heart that is in control of each one. From this, we can see that desire cannot lead us to success or understanding.

Wenzi, "Talismanic Words" ⓣ

169 | Good instruction

Kind words are not as good
  as kind sounds that enter deeply.
Good politics is not as good
  as good instructions to the people.
The people fear "good" politics,
while they love good instruction.
"Good" politics takes the people's wealth.
Good instructions earns the people's hearts.

Mengzi, "Jin Xin I" ©

170 | Escaping the net

Rock and fire go like lightning,
conjugal love always causes suffering.
If one realizes the nature of true and false,
one extinguishes sin, clears the heart, and escapes the net.

Anonymous, ancient Buddhist verse Ⓑ

171 | The fire within most of us

Rub two sticks together: they burn. Heat metal: it melts. When yin and yang move apart, heaven and earth are greatly disturbed. There will be thunderstorm upon thunderstorm, fire within rain, and all the locust trees will burn down.

There are worse situations: we are often caught between two sides from which we cannot escape. Like a chrysalis, we can achieve nothing. Our hearts are caught in the space between heaven and earth. We are caught between comfort and gloominess. The sticks of our profit and loss rub together and ignite a great fire.

The majority of people burn like this too. It grows more ferocious by the month and they can never overcome this fire. When this fire burns continually, then their Tao is lost.

Zhuangzi, "External Matters" ⓣ

172 | Benevolence first, ritual after

When benevolence is established in a ruler's heart, then understanding is the servant and ritual is its completion. Therefore, a king puts benevolence first and ritual after, matching how heaven bestows.

Xunzi, "Grand Digest" ©

173 | Bring benefit to the people

Laozi said: If a child dies for the sake of parents, or a citizen dies for the sake of their sovereign, it's not because they want to be famous but because they hold so much kindness in their hearts that they will not be deterred by hard choices.

Similarly, the noble one is concerned and worried over any failure to support what's proper. That feeling is within them and so they examine circumstances and then act.

The sage is unashamed of shadows, the noble one is careful to act independently. They look beyond the short-term to the long-term.

Thus, when the sages are in charge, they follow what's expressed in folk music to govern people. In contrast, lesser leaders want people to admire them for their thoughts.

Ambition must never override the need to bring benefit to people.

Wenzi, "Sincerity" ⓣ

THE WAY OF HEART & BEAUTY

174 | At the pond shore

At the pond shore
of reeds and lotuses
is a beautiful one,
shapely and fair.
Awake or asleep,
I can do nothing—
so anxious in my heart.

Classic of Poetry, "Ze Po" ©

175 | The duke's dream

Song Yuan Jun dreamed in the middle of the night that a man with disheveled hair peered at him through the door and said: "I have come from the abyss of Zailu, commissioned by the Pure River to go the Count of the River, but the fisherman Yue Qie has caught me."

When Duke Yuan awoke, he summoned his diviner.

When the diviner had performed his calculations, he said: "It is a divine tortoise."

The duke asked if there was a fisherman named Yue Qie and his attendants replied that there was. He ordered the man to come to court the next morning. Accordingly, Yue Qie appeared the next day.

"What have you caught?" asked the duke.

"I caught a white tortoise some five units round."

"Present that tortoise."

151

As soon as the tortoise arrived, the duke could not decide whether to kill it or to let it live. He was unsure in his heart. So he turned again to divination and the reading was: "Kill the tortoise and use its shell for divination."

The attendants killed the tortoise and hollowed it out. They drilled seventy-two holes in its shell and not a single divining slip that resulted was wrong.

Zhongni commented: "This divine tortoise could appear in a dream to Duke Yuan, but it could not avoid the net of Yue Qie. Its wisdom allowed seventy-two perforations to divine without a single error, and yet it could not avoid the agony of having its bowels scooped out. And so, we see that wisdom has its difficulties, and divine power has its failures. Even if one reaches great wisdom, ten thousand people scheme in opposition. Fish do not fear the net, they fear the pelican.

"Put away your small wisdom and your great wisdom will be bright. Put away your excellence and let your natural excellence come forward. When a child is born they do not need a great master and yet they learn to speak: they are able to speak just from living where they are.

"A penetrating eye brings clarity. An acute ear brings hearing. A discriminating nose brings shivers of recognition. A discerning mouth brings sweet taste. A pervasive heart brings wisdom. A permeating wisdom brings virtue. All in all, Tao does not want obstruction. Obstructions produce blockage. Unending blockage stops all progress, and massive disasters arise.

"All creatures have a wisdom upon which they rely. If they don't flourish, it is not the fault of heaven. Heaven per-

meates them with it endlessly both day and night. Only people close themselves off to this.

"The womb is a marvelous space. The heart holds all the movements of heaven. If a house doesn't have enough rooms, then wife and mother-in-law argue. If the heart doesn't hold heaven's movements, then the six kinds of perception clash with each other.

"The great forests, hills, and mountains are perfect over people only because we can't overcome their divinity."

Zhuangzi, "External Matters" ⊤

176 | The tortoise in the ancestral temple

Zhuangzi was fishing on the banks of the Pu River when the King of Chu sent two envoys with this message: "I wish to trouble you with ruling the nation."

Zhuangzi held his rod steady and said without turning: "I have heard that there is a divine tortoise shell in Chu and that the animal died three thousand years ago. The king stores this shell in a special wicker basket within his ancestral temple. Do you suppose it was better for the tortoise to die and have its shell venerated during grand ceremonies? Or would it have been better for it to live to drag its tail in the mud?"

"We suppose that it would have been better for it to have lived to drag its tail in the mud," answered the two envoys.

"Go then! I will drag my tail in the mud."

Zhuangzi, "Autumn Floods" ⊤

177 | What goes along with being good

Those who are moral, smart, artistic, and wise
are always pained and sick.
They are the lonely subordinates, the children of
          concubines.
They hold their hearts against peril.
They worry deeply.
    That's because they're intelligent.

Mengzi, "Jin Xin I" ©

178 | Let no state invade another

Let a small country
keep a small population,
and have a supply of goods
ten- or a hundredfold more
than people can use.
Let the people weigh death
and not migrate far.

While they would have boats and carts,
they wouldn't ride them.
While they would have armor and weapons,
they wouldn't show them.

Let them return to
tallying with knotted cords,

sweet food,
beautiful clothes,
restful dwellings,
and joyful customs.

Let neighboring countries see each other,
and hear one another's chickens and dog,
but to old age,
even to death,
let no state invade another.

Daodejing, 80 Ⓣ

179 | A person is a microcosm of heaven and earth

Laozi said: People receive the changes of heaven and earth and so are born.

In the first month, an embryo is soft and slight. In the second month, blood vessels form. In the third month, there is quickening. In the fourth month, a fetus forms. In the fifth month, it has limbs. In the six month, it has bones. In the seventh month, its body has formed. In the eighth month, it moves. In the ninth month, the baby seems impatient to be born. And in the tenth month, birth occurs.

A human body is then complete. Its organs are intact. The liver corresponds to the eyes. The kidneys correspond to the ears. The spleen corresponds to the tongue. The lungs correspond to the nose. The gallbladder corresponds to the mouth. We have an outer skin. We have inner membranes.

Our heads are part of the way of heaven, our feet are set squarely upon the earth.

Heaven has the four seasons, the Five Phases, the Solution of Nine, and 360 days. A human being has four limbs, five organs, nine orifices, and 360 joints.

Heaven has wind, rain, cold, and hot. A human being has give and take, joy and anger. The gallbladder corresponds to the cloud. The lungs correspond to the air. The spleen corresponds to the wind. The kidneys correspond to the rain. The liver corresponds to the thunder. Human beings are a microcosm of heaven and earth, with the heart acting as the master.

The eyes and ears are like the sun and moon. Blood and breath are like the wind and rain. If the sun and moon no longer moved, then they would be eclipsed and there would be no light. If the wind and rain did not come in a timely way, there would be destruction, collapse, and numerous calamities. If the stars did not revolve, the states and nations would suffer disaster.

The Tao of heaven and earth is on a scale that is great and large, and yet it still has integrity and is orderly in its brightness. Love is its spiritual radiance.

Could people's ears and eyes continue so long without break? Could their minds and spirits keep moving without any faltering? This is why the sages guard the inner and keep the outer.

Wenzi, "Nine Guardings" ⑦

180 | What can I do?

The crows flap away.
They return in a flock.
Everyone is good.
I alone am miserable.
How did I offend heaven?
What crime was it?
My heart is so sad.
What can I do?

Classic of Poetry, "Xiao Bian" ©

181 | Choosing poverty over fame

Zengzi lived in Wei with a hemp cloak and nothing else. His face was taut and lean, his hands and feet were rough and calloused, and he could only afford to light a fire every three days. For ten years he did not buy new clothes. If he straightened his cap, the cords broke. If he tugged at his collar, his elbows stuck out. When he wore his shoes, his heels showed. Still, he tied his hair and sang the *Odes of Shang* with a voice that filled heaven and earth as clearly as bells and chimes.

The Son of Heaven could not persuade him to become a minister. The rulers of the vassal states could not get him to favor them.

Therefore, when nourishing one's purpose, the body is forgotten. When nourishing the body, gain is forgotten. When attaining Tao, the heart is forgotten.

Zhuangzi, "The Resigning Kings" ①

157

182 | On the march home

When we first set out
the willows were fresh and green.
Now we head back and I think
how rain and snow will be falling
and how long and slow the march.
My heart is wounded and sad:
no one knows how it aches.

Classic of Poetry, "Cai Wei" ©

183 | Anything sought can be found

Laozi said: Those who are called sages are peaceful in their places and accord with their times. They are glad in their deeds as is appropriate to their era.

Our sorrows and joys, the sins against virtue, and our likes and dislikes all strain our hearts. Delight and anger are excesses in Tao. We are born as part of heaven's course and we die as a part of the transformation of things.

Stillness combined with yin is virtue, and movement together with yang becomes the same wave. Therefore, the heart must be the master of such appearances and the sacred must be treasured in one's heart.

When our bodies are worked endlessly, we collapse. When we employ our vitality endlessly, we are exhausted. The sages heed this and do not dare go to excess. They use

nonbeing to respond to being; investigate patterns; use emptiness to receive solidity; will persist in integrity; and are content in emptiness and stillness to the end of their lives. They do not harden themselves to anyone nor do they favor anyone. Embracing virtue and fusing harmony, they are obedient to heaven, meet with Tao, and stay close to virtue. They begin nothing for profit, and do nothing to advance misfortune. They are indifferent to their own death or life, and so can be said to have reached the spiritual.

Spirituality is to find what you seek and to complete what you do.

Wenzi, "Nine Guardings" ⑦

184 | There will never be so much . . .

Laozi said: Treat heaven and earth lightly and your soul won't tire. Treat all things delicately and your heart will fill with confidence. Treat life and death evenly and your thoughts will be fearless. Treat all change with equanimity and your understanding will never be dazzled.

Realized people brace themselves upon an unshakable pillar. No barriers block their routes when they travel. Nothing stops them from giving to their community. Nothing keeps them from learning the eternal teachings. No past will prevent them from getting their way. Nothing will ever be blocked, bent, straightened, lowered, or pulled up. No doubts will keep them from embracing life, despite the disasters and happiness, or of gain and loss.

There will never be so much that the heart suffers.

The righteous relieve oppression through benevolence. They never allow their armies to loot and plunder and are strict, upright, and just. They will not baselessly seek gain—a noble one will die for righteousness. They will not dwell on riches and honor either—they never fear death for the sake of righteousness. Again, the situation lies in nonaction. Nonaction means no stress. It means imposing no oppressive work on others—a reminder of the image of the unshakable pillar.

On a higher level, the realized person's contemplation brings coherence and the thoughts of deep and primary virtue in Tao. On a lower level, they investigate by walking in the profane world to the point that they become reserved. Nonaction for the sake of the world sets the drumbeat of learning.

Wenzi, "Nine Guardings" ⑦

185 | The root of the heart

The noble one might want vast territories
and millions of citizens,
but they will not be happy.

A noble one might think joy
is being at the center of the world
deciding for everyone within the four seas,
but their own nature will not thrive.

Great deeds do not add to a noble one's nature,
just as poverty and low dwelling don't diminish it.
Such apportionments are already fixed.

The nature of a noble one
is kindness, righteousness, propriety, and wisdom:
that is the root of the heart.

Then a lively appearance,
clear-eyed expression,
and strong posture out to the four limbs—
all emerge without being told.

Mengzi, "Jin Xin I" ©

The kui-demon envies the millipede. The millipede envies the snake. The snake envies the wind. The wind envies the eye. The eye envies the heart.

"I must hop on one leg to go anywhere," the kui-demon said to the millipede. I'm not like you. You have so many legs. How is it that you are so special?"

"This isn't so," said the millipede. "Have you seen a creature that can spit? It can spurt a large gob like a pearl followed by a spray-like mist. Now, I move by heaven's machinery, but I don't know why that is so."

"I move by many feet," the millipede said to the snake, "but I can't keep up with you that have no feet. Why is that?"

"We are moved by heaven's machinery. How can that be changed? I don't need feet."

"I move by means of my spine and ribs," the snake said to the wind. "But at least I have an appearance. Now, you, sir, roar off the Northern Sea to the Southern Sea without needing a body. How is that?"

"Just so," said the wind. "Perhaps I can charge from the Northern Sea to the Southern Sea, but you can point at me, and are therefore better off than me. You can also walk on me, and so you're also better than me there too. Nevertheless, I can snap trees and blow down large buildings. Only I can do that. Therefore, where the numbers are few, there is no prevailing. Where the numbers are great, then all can be overcome. But for the greatest of victories, only the sage is capable of that."

Zhuangzi, "Autumn Floods" ⑦

187 | Abandon cleverness

Laozi said: Honor, power, and ample benefit is what people truly covet, but those are insignificant when compared to preserving oneself.

Therefore, the sage eats just enough to be full; fills their empty lungs enough to breathe; dresses just enough not to be cold; and fits their emotions to the situation without excessiveness. They have no voracious desires to get anything. They don't amass much. Their eyes are pure—not searching. Their ears are serene—not eavesdropping. Their mouths stay silent. They trust their hearts and are not anxious.

Abandon cleverness. Revert to the supremely plain. Cease your thoughts. Get rid of knowledge and reason. Have no likes or dislikes. This is called great openness. Rid yourself of filth and strain; there will be nothing like what has yet to run its course. If you feel all this, what action won't succeed?

Know the harmony of wellness—that is, do not worry about getting some advantage. Clear yourself inside and outside of any mark and you will not be tempted to use power.

When nothing is beyond the outermost, one reaches greatness. When nothing is more inner than the innermost, one reaches the precious. If you know great preciousness, where can you go and not succeed?

Wenzi, "Nine Guardings" ⑦

188 | Compassionate hands

If we can change our minds,
  that's Buddhahood.

Spring comes and the mountain flowers everywhere.
So we have a pair of compassionate hands
to touch and temper the hearts of all people.

Baiyun Shouduan (1025–1072), "Compassionate Hands" Ⓑ

189 | Learn without knowing

Laozi said: Those who are called True Persons have characters that accord with Tao. They have, but seem to have-not.
They are solid, but seem to be empty. They control what is
within them, and don't try to control what is outside them.
They understand supreme plainness, nonaction, as well as
returning to simplicity.

Their bodies fundamentally enclose their spirits because
they walk at the root of heaven and earth, beyond the chaff
of falsity, grime, and dust. They are free, unfettered, because
their business is to have nothing that they must do, no mach-
inations, and no knowledge for the sake of opportunity. They
don't carry any of this in their hearts.

They examine carefully so that there is no falsity and are
not moved by things. Watchful of how things change, they
yet guard their purpose and keep their heart's intentions
focused and inside themselves. They understand clearly that

disaster and happiness are one. They live in place without wondering why they are doing so. They conduct themselves without calculating outcomes. They learn without knowing, do not scrutinize and yet still see, engage in nonaction and yet still succeed, and refuse to rule and instead encourage discussion. They have feelings and yet are proper, shy but emotional, and they are accepting where there is no other alternative. When it's time to shine, they are brilliant. When it's time for shadows, they are effective. All this, they do by following Tao.

Wenzi, "Nine Guardings"

190 | Chant

To chant the name of Buddha is easy; to have a faithful heart
is hard.

The heart and mouth usually are not as one and are always
idle.
If the mouth chants "Amitabha," but the heart is scattered,
even shouting will wear the throat in vain.

Hanshan Deqing (1546–1623), "The Heart and Mouth Combined as One" Ⓑ

191 | The influence of music

The kings of the ancient days had enormous responsibilities.
So they had rules to channel their sorrow. They had rules to
shape their happiness too. Whether it was grief or joy, they
set boundaries. Everybody used the rites in all aspects of
their lives.

The sages saw that music brought joy and that it improved
the hearts of all people. It expressed the deepest feelings, and
it influenced attitudes and customs, which were always in
flux. That's why the kings of ancient days put such an emphasis on music and made sure it was taught.

Book of Rites, "Yue Ji" ©

192 | All song comes from the heart

All song comes from the heart
and all movement from the heart is natural.
Emotion moves the body,
and our body makes sound.
We vary those sounds and find tones,
and use those tones to make music.

Book of Rites, "Yue Ji" ©

193 | How to study

Your mouth chants,
your heart retains
this in morning,
this in evening.

Three Character Classic Ⓛ

194 | What harms the heart as much as the body?

If you're starving, you want delicious food.
If you're thirsty, you want good drink.
But that's not all there is
to starvation and thirst being harmful.

It's not only your mouth and belly
that are harmed by starvation and thirst;
your heart will also be harmed.

Mengzi, "Jin Xin I" Ⓒ

195 | Attend to inner nature

Laozi said: The ancients who followed Tao attended to their inner natures. They managed their hearts artfully, nurtured themselves through harmony, and maintained what was suitable. Happy in Tao, they were not bothered by being lowly, and content in their virtue, they were not bothered by being poor.

They didn't try to get anything that their inner natures did not want. They did not do anything that made their hearts unhappy. They did not strain their virtue to bring profit to their inner natures. They did not lose their peacefulness over what merely made life easy. They did not throw or jump willfully but were systematic and regulated. They could enact the world's ceremonies.

They apportioned their food when eating; controlled their appearance when dressing; found a fitting home for dwelling; kept their feeling suitable in their conduct; gave surplus to the world rather than keep it for themselves; and they could be entrusted with all living beings without seeking advantage for themselves. Why would they bother with being poor or rich, noble or lowly, or even worry about the loss of life?

Since they were forever so, they could be said to embody Tao!

Wenzi, "Nine Guardings" Ⓣ

196 | If you want to nourish your heart

If you want to nourish your heart,
nothing is better than to reduce your wants.

If you have few desires,
you might miss some things,
but they will be few.

If you have many desires,
you may gain some things,
but they will be few.

Mengzi, "Jin Xin II" ©

197 | If you want to right the world

Laozi said: People receive their energy from heaven. The ears
and eyes sense sound and color; the nose and mouth sense
the fragrant and foul; the skin senses cold and warm. Each
one of us has these feelings. Through them, some die, some
live, some become noble ones, and some become petty people. We think that's because there are different ways to control ourselves.

The spirit has deep knowledge. The spirit seems color-
lessly pure, but it has wisdom and understanding. Knowledge is the seat of the heart. When knowledge is fair, then the
heart is at peace.

No one views rushing floodwaters as an example of limpid waters, and that applies to viewing one's own purity: it

takes stillness. One can only see one's own spiritual purity when thoughts are placid. Only then can you see the true shape of things.

Therefore, use this to see the false and the useless. Use a mirror to illuminate the dusty and filthy. Use the spirit to make lusts and errors distinct. Then your heart will be realized. Moreover when the spirit is thus so emotionally present, one returns to emptiness. Then impetuousness vanishes as one collects and stores the energy of one's breath. This is the goal of the sages' search.

If you want to right the world, secure your own life and character first.

Wenzi, "Nine Guardings" Ⓣ

198 | Two views of the heart as a mirror

The body is a bodhi tree,
the heart is a bright mirror on its stand.
Polish it constantly and often,
and don't allow dust to collect.

Yuquan Shenxiu (606–706), *The Platform Sutra of the Sixth Patriarch* Ⓑ

The bodhi (i.e., enlightenment) at root is not a tree.
A bright mirror also has no stand.
Originally, there was not a thing:
so where could dust settle?

Dajian Huineng (638–713), *The Platform Sutra of the Sixth Patriarch* Ⓑ

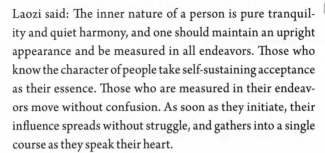

199 | See the root but know the tips

Laozi said: The inner nature of a person is pure tranquility and quiet harmony, and one should maintain an upright appearance and be measured in all endeavors. Those who know the character of people take self-sustaining acceptance as their essence. Those who are measured in their endeavors move without confusion. As soon as they initiate, their influence spreads without struggle, and gathers into a single course as they speak their heart.

See the root, but know the tips of the branches. Hold ten thousand obligations within one grasp. Speak with skillfully accumulated knowledge; be aware of what you do and learn as you move. Know when to move and when to stop. This is called Tao.

A strong heart makes others praise you as lofty and virtuous. An excessive heart makes others denigrate you as base and low. Once words leave your mouth, you can't stop them from reaching others. Once you act, nothing at hand will stop it from reaching far.

Anything is difficult to finish, while failure is easy. Reputation is difficult to establish while toppling is easy. Ordinary people always act lightly to reduce harm and make their work easy and slight—to the point that they suffer misfortune.

Disaster reaches us by itself. Happiness reaches fullness by itself. Misfortune and good fortune emerge from the same gate, and benefit and harm are neighbors. For this not to happen to us is, in essence, impossible to separate.

Consequently, it is wise to consider the door to disaster and happiness, the difference between movement and stillness, the alternations of advantage and disadvantage.

You must examine this with care.

Wenzi, "Abstruse Understanding" ⓣ

200 | Carving wood into a sacrificial vessel

Take a block of a one-hundred-year-old tree and make a sacrificial vessel from it. Paint it green and yellow. Throw the waste wood into the dump.

Compare the sacrificial vessel with what's lying in the dump. You might say that they differ in beauty and ugliness—but they have both lost their essential nature.

Zhuangzi, "Heaven and Earth" ⓣ

201 | Perfecting the beauty in others

The noble one perfects the beauty in others,
and does not reinforce their faults.
Inferior people do the opposite.

Analects, "Yan Yuan" ©

Zhuangzi had entered the boundary of Eagle Hill when a strange bird flew in from the south. Its wings were seven measures wide, and its big eyes measured several inches. It circled around, dipped, and landed in a grove of chestnut trees.

"What kind of bird is that?" Zhuangzi asked himself. "It has large wings, but it doesn't fly away. It has large eyes, but it doesn't notice me!" He tied back his robes, fit a pellet to his sling, took his stance, and waited for a chance to shoot.

Just then, a cicada landed in a beautifully shady spot, paying no attention to itself. A mantis sprang from hiding to seize it. It was so intent on its prey that it forgot about its own safety. The strange bird swooped down and ate them both.

Seeing how the benefit of one came from the negligence of another, Zhuangzi paused and said: "Ah, one action leads to another, and any two things can then be caught in turn."

He put away his sling and pellet and was turning to leave when the forester rushed up to accuse him of poaching.

Zhuangzi, "Mountain Tree" ⓣ

THE
WAY
OF
H
E
A
R
T
&
B
E
A
U
T
Y

THE
WAY
OF
H
E
A
R
T
&
B
E
A
U
T
Y

Laozi said: Those who are called sages find what's suitable to their nature and nothing more. They are measured in what they eat, limit the appearance of what they wear, and regulate themselves. They don't allow desire or corruption to start in their hearts. Therefore, they can lead the world because they only do what is for the world's sake. They can accept fame and honor because they are not excessive in their conduct and seek nothing for themselves. They are sincere in communicating life's sentiments: benevolence, righteousness, reason, and closeness.

It seems that if one's spirit is unblocked, one's heart is unburdened, communications are clear and open, tranquility is undisturbed, arrogance does not tempt, sound and color do not lead to lasciviousness, arguments are not verbalized, knowledge does not lead to interference, and courage is not undone by fear, then the True Person can move freely.

Whatever is born is born from what was never-born. What changes has changed from what never changes. You cannot attain this Tao by trying for a knowledge that encompasses heaven and earth or is as bright and shining as the sun and moon; or by any chain of logic, or by discussions as solid as metal and stone. None of that will help the world.

Of this, the sage is always vigilant.

Wenzi, "Nine Guardings" ⓣ

204 | What makes our hearts wild

The five colors make us blind.
The five tones make us deaf.
The five flavors dull our taste.
Hurry, haste, and pursuit
make our hearts go wild.
Coveting rare goods
hobbles our walk.

Therefore, wise people provide
for bellies and not eyes.
They leave one and choose the other.

Daodejing, 12 ⓣ

205 | What lowers the high and raises the low

The Tao of heaven lowers the high and raises the low. It lowers the abundant and elevates the deficient. The rivers and seas are where the earth is low, and that's why the world responds by honoring them. The sages stay humble and modest, peaceful and quiet, reserved and yielding—this is to see the lowly. With modest hearts, with no attempts to possess—this is to see the lacking. To see what's lowly is to find the delicate bits that lead to the high. To see the lacking is to become a great person.

Boasting will never stand. Extravagance will never last long. Bullies will die. The overflowing will drain away.

Whirlwinds and rainstorms won't last a day. Even a small valley won't be flooded in a flash by the most violent and powerful downpours. Whatever cannot last a long time will be extinguished. The small valley is the place where the violent and powerful drain away.

Therefore the sage keeps to the female; gets rid of extravagance and arrogance; and never dares to behave with the air of a bully.

Whoever can stay with the force of the female and the valley and also establish themselves with the force of the male and the hills without extravagance and arrogance can therefore last long.

Wenzi, "Nine Guardings" ⓣ

206 | Reject attachment

"Let's please talk more," Confucius said.

"To understand what is," Laozi said, "we must reach beauty to reach contentment. Once we reach beauty, while still traveling in this world, we reach contentment. Such a person is called a Realized Person."

"Is there a method to achieve this?"

"Grass-eating animals don't like to change their pastures. Water-dwelling creatures don't like to change their waters. They'll tolerate small changes, but they cannot accept anything that is contrary to their primary needs.

"Joy, anger, sadness, contentment—these emotions don't enter their considerations. All creatures share the same world. As long as they can all share as one, then whether of four limbs or the hundred kinds of bodies, they are mere dust and dirt. Death and life, endings and beginnings are like the succession of day and night—impossible to evade. Furthermore, gain and loss, bad and good fortune all come in between.

"Reject attachment as you would reject being splattered with mud. Understand instead the attachment to yourself. The value of being myself is not destroyed by any of life's changes. Besides, there may be ten thousand changes before there is any result. What's important enough to trouble our heart? That is the explanation of Tao!"

Zhuangzi, "Tian Zifang" ⑦

207 | Everything is mysteriously joined

Laozi said: The sages enclose themselves in yin and they open themselves in yang. They have reached the point where nothing makes them happy and nothing makes them unhappy. Since nothing makes them unhappy, they have reached the pinnacle of happiness.

It's a matter of inner happiness that goes outward, rather than of outer happiness that goes inward. Therefore, those who have their own happiness also know their own purpose and worth in the world. It's natural. This should be taken as vitally important by the world.

This isn't up to anyone else; it's up to me. It isn't in other people, it's inside my own self. Once the self reaches this point, the ten thousand things will follow. Therefore, those who attain the art and understanding of the heart regard fondness and lust, likes and dislikes as external. That is why they have no joy, no anger, no happiness, no suffering. Everything is mysteriously joined and beyond wrong and right.

Wenzi, "Nine Guardings" Ⓣ

208 | The one breath

All creatures deem life to be
beautiful, divine, and wonderful.
They deem death to be
putrid and rotten.

But the putrid and rotten transforms
into the divine and wonderful.
The divine and wonderful transforms
into the putrid and rotten.

Therefore, it is said:
"For all under heaven, there is one breath
and the sage prizes that oneness."

Zhuangzi, "Knowledge from Northern Wanderings" Ⓣ

209 | Poem to abstain from killing

Bloody meat: juicy, aromatic delicacy—
hard to consider pain, suffering, and agony.
What if you were in their place? What thoughts would your
      heart hold?
Who would agree to have their own body cut with a knife?

Lu You (1125–1210), *Collation and Annotation of Jinnan Poetry* Ⓑ

210 | Mourning with complete love

Calling your lost one's soul back
is the Tao of complete love.
You pray and make offerings in your heart,
look through every dark region,
question every ghost and spirit on the road.
You face north, you search every darkness—
it is the proper thing to do.

You put offerings in plain vessels,
because the hearts of the living
are filled with pure sorrow.
In all the rites of sacrifice and mourning,
you do your utmost just like that.
Do you know if the spirit will come?
You must be guided by your pure and reverent heart.

Book of Rites, "Tan Gong II" Ⓒ

211 | Better than being incorruptible

Laozi said: To trust officials with the division of wealth is not as good as setting predetermined amounts and drawing lots. Why is that? Even a heart inclined toward fairness is not as good as having no heart involved at all.

To trust incorruptible officials with guarding wealth is not as good as locking a door and sealing it. That's because the desire-for-being-incorruptible is not as good as having no desire at all.

If you hold up people's flaws, they'll blame you. But if they see their own ugliness in a mirror, they will be pleased. If people can deal with things instead of themselves, then they won't wear themselves out.

Wenzi, "Talismanic Words" ⑦

212 | What we really want

Drinking, eating, and sex is what people really want.
Death, loneliness, poverty, and hardship is what people
      really fear.
Thus, desire and fear are the two extremes of the heart.
We keep them hidden in our hearts,
where no one can guess or measure.
Beauty and ugliness are invisible in all our hearts.
If we wanted unity and sparingness,
shouldn't we stay with propriety?

Book of Rites, "Li Yun" ©

Xu Wugui (No Ghost) visited Lord Wu (Martial). Lord Wu said: "You, sir, have been living in the mountain forests, eating acorns and chestnuts, and subsisting on onions and chives without deigning to visit this royal person. Now you've come. Is it because you've become old? Do you once again want to taste wine and meat? Or have you come to bless the royal Altar of Land and Grain?"

"I, Wugui, was born in poverty and squalor, and I have never tasted the wine and meat of you, my lord. I have come to save your highness."

"What's that? You've come to save me?"

"I've come to save your spirit and your body."

"What do you mean?"

"Heaven and earth nourishes all creatures as one. One who rises high may not be excellent. One living low may not be lacking. Your highness is indeed the lord of ten thousand chariots, but you impose hardship on an entire nation of people to please your ears, eyes, nose, and mouth. But this isn't true to your spirit. Your spirit wants goodness and harmony and deplores debauchery. Such indulgence is a sickness. That's why you need saving. Why is your highness the only one with this sickness?"

"I've long wanted to see you," said Lord Wu. "I want to love my people and righteously end all war. Is that possible?"

"No, sire, you cannot proceed that way. To love the people is the first step toward hurting them. Righteousness is the root of war. If your majesty proceeds, you are unlikely to be successful. Every contrived attempt to achieve beauty is bad. Even if you act with benevolence and righteousness, it will be artificial from the start! You may begin with an idea and attempt the form, but anything you accomplish will lead to conflict. Your highness must not mass soldiers in your elegant towers or allow infantrymen and horsemen near your palace altar. Banish any thought that is contrary to success. Dismiss clever plans to conquer others. Abandon all schemes to conquer others. Reject using war to conquer others.

"If I were to kill another state's citizens and officials, capture its people, and take its land, I might satisfy my personal wants, but would my spirit recognize the war as good? Isn't there harm in every victory? Instead, cultivate the sincerity in your chest, do as you feel is consistent with heaven and earth and never vary from that. Your people will have already escaped death. Then your highness will need no artifice to bring about an end to war!"

Zhuangzi, "Xu Wugui" Ⓣ

214 | The two kinds of hearts

Laozi said: People don't have the same energies in their hearts. An orderly heart operates with positive energy; a disordered heart flows with contentious energy.

Whether a heart is orderly or disorderly lies in whether it follows Tao and virtue. If it is with Tao, the heart is under control. If it loses Tao, then it is confused.

An orderly heart is deferential in interactions with other people. A disorderly heart will conflict in interaction with other people. Deference leads to virtue. Conflict leads to deceit and betrayal. Virtuousness leads to positive energy. Deceit and betrayal lead to the flow of contentious energy.

Those with positive energy humble themselves and respect people. Those with contentious energy humiliate others and demand respect for themselves. These two energies can only be controlled through Tao.

The Tao of heaven is like an echo: its response is immediate. Amassed virtue leads to happiness and life. Amassed disasters lead to growing blame: then governance becomes bureaucracy; filial piety declines for the sake of one's spouse; suffering is born out of concern and division; and illness returns mightily after healing.

Therefore, it's said: "If you are as careful at the end as you are at the beginning, then none of your endeavors will fail."

Wenzi, "Talismanic Words" Ⓣ

215 | Heaven and earth are beautiful

Heaven and earth are beautiful
    —no one needs to mention it.
The four seasons follow each other clearly
    —no one needs to discuss it.
All creatures are complete in their principles
    —no one needs to explain it.

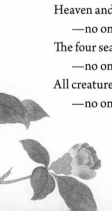

The sages see the source of heaven and earth's beauty
and the principles of all creatures.
That's why realized people like them do nothing.

A great sage doesn't try to make anything—
because they see heaven and earth.

Now, marvelously enlightened, understanding the essence
throughout hundreds of transformations,
they see that all creatures remain unaware
of death and life, square and round,
and do not know their own root,
even if they continue to exist from old.

All within the six directions is vast.
Nothing is separated within it.
Even to the smallest autumn hair,
everything is complete within it.

It contains all under heaven without exception;
each body needs nothing else.
Yin and yang and the four seasons move within it,
each one has its proper sequence.
Whether seemingly confused or through destruction,
all continues to exists.
Whether seemingly elusive or formless,
there is nevertheless a spirit.

The ten thousand things and the animals
remain unaware of any of this,
yet this is called the basis and root.

It is through this, that we
can observe heaven.

Zhuangzi, "Knowledge from Northern Wanderings" ⑦

216 | What's natural

Laozi said: The Tao of heaven and earth relies on virtue. The action of Tao in life is by means of each thing having reached its own subtle internal rightness—without needing arrangement or expense, without needing any effort to establish, without needing position or recognition, without needing fame and prominence, without needing gifts or property, and without needing to use military force.

Therefore, Tao stands without needing to be taught. It should be clearly illuminated without needing examination. When we say that Tao stands without needing to be taught it means it does not try to wrest control of people's abilities. That it should be clearly illuminated without needing to be examined means not to harm any of the people's affairs.

Those who teach Tao counter virtue and harm other beings. Therefore, yin and yang; the four seasons; metal, wood, water, fire, earth all have the same Tao, although they have different patterns. The ten thousand things are the same in character, but they are different in form.

Wise people don't teach each other. The capable aren't beholden to each other. When the sage establishes the law, they did so by guiding the people's hearts and made each one natural. Then a person while alive needed no favors and their deaths were blameless.

Heaven and earth are not kind; they take all things as straw dogs. The sages are not kind; they take all people as straw dogs. People who are compassionate, loving, benevolent, and righteous, are of a close and narrow Tao. The narrow enters the great but is confused. The close travel far and are lost. The sages' Tao enters the great but is not confused, travels far but is not lose. Constancy is emptiness, preserving oneself is the ultimate act. That is called divine virtue.

Wenzi, "Natural" ⓣ

217 | When the world was disordered

The world was in complete disorder. Worthy and holy people did not shine. The virtue of Tao was not whole, and so many in the world got a partial glimpse and took it as best for themselves. It was comparable to the ear, eye, nose, and mouth—each able but none communicating together. So it was with the hundred schools and the multitude of able people. Each one had its own excellence, each had some proper time for use, but even so none was fundamental or covered everything. Take the case of a scholar who judges what's beautiful in heaven and earth, distinguishes the principles behind the ten thousand things, and who investigates all the ancients. Few can perfect themselves toward the beauty of heaven and earth or explain appearances with spiritual clarity. Thus it

was that the Tao, with the sage in inner matters and the king in outer matters, darkened and no longer shined. It became turgid and it no longer produced.

Everyone in the world did as they wanted and acted only for themselves. How sad! The hundred schools were lost and did not return or try to work together. Unfortunately, the students of a later age no longer saw the purity of heaven and earth or the great body of work left by the ancients. The art of Tao was fractured and the parts were scattered throughout the world.

Zhuangzi, "Under Heaven" ⑦

218 | Understanding tranquility

Laozi said: Tranquility is the ruler. It is harmonious, reasonable, quiet, and does not interfere with others. It is plain, simple, and unsophisticated. Calm and serene, nothing is done impatiently with others; instead all is in accord with Tao.

Outwardly, it keeps a sense of common righteousness. Words have forethought and reason. Actions are for the sake of delight and emotions matter.

One's heart is peaceful and never pretends. One is plain in all matters, never elaborate, and never hides anything. Never scheming in the beginning, never manipulative to the end, one is peaceful whether on approach or on remaining, whether sudden or steadily moving. One is pervasive with the whole of heaven and earth; of the same processes as yin and yang; harmonizes as one with the four seasons; as bright and forthright as the sun and moon; and one keeps with the changes of Tao for the sake other people. Cunning, swindling, lying—one never allows these in one's heart.

This is how heaven covers us with virtue, and earth supports us with happiness: The four seasons stay in sequence. The wind and rain are not oppressive. The sun and moon are tranquil and yet they rise brightly. The Five Stars never fail to orbit.

This is the understanding of tranquility.

Wenzi, "Lower Virtue" ⓣ

219 | On emptiness, from the *Heart Sutra*

It is thus that no appearances are within emptiness:
>No sensation, perception, volition, or consciousness.
>No eye, ear, nose, tongue, body, or mind.
>No sight, sound, scent, taste, touch, or thought.
>No ken and even no consciousness.
>Nothing is not understood, nor is there an end to
>>delusion.
>No aging and death, nor end of aging and death.
>No suffering, origin, cessation, or Tao.
>No wisdom and no attainment.

Because nothing is to be attained,
bodhisattvas maintain *prajnaparamita*.

Then their hearts are without hindrance.
Since they are without hindrance, they are without fear.
They escape inverted dream thoughts,
and completely realize nirvana.

Prajnaparamita Heart Sutra Ⓑ

220 | Good fortune will come

Laozi said: Don't seek actions that could be blameworthy. Don't resent others who criticize you. Cultivate yourself enough to earn praiseworthy virtue instead of seeking praise for yourself.

You can do nothing to stave off disaster. Believe in yourself even if you don't know about it. You can do nothing to ensure good fortune. Believe in yourself even if good doesn't come right away.

Disasters will occur, criticism will come, but even if you're exhausted, do not worry. Good fortune will come and the accusations will end.

Therefore, remain clear and don't feel sorry for yourself. Lead a quiet and peaceful life with a happy heart and keep control through nonaction.

Wenzi, "Nine Guardings" Ⓣ

221 | On a journey of ten thousand miles

On a journey of ten thousand miles, blown by sandstorms.
North, south, east, and west, it's all home.
My chest ends up hollow and trembling.
I gaze in stillness: my heart is a white lotus.

Yelu Chucai (1190–1244), "On a Journey of Ten Thousand Miles" Ⓑ

222 | Having no fixed heart

Wise people have no fixed hearts,
but take the hearts of the people as their own.
To those who are good to me,
　　I am good.
To those who are bad to me,
　　I am also good.
That's good virtue.
To those who are sincere to me,
　　I am sincere.
To those who are insincere to me,
　　I am also sincere.
That's sincere virtue.
The wise people are at peace with the world
　　and they keep their hearts obscure.
But the people keep their eyes and ears on them,
　　and the wise people treat everyone as their children.

Daodejing, 49 Ⓣ

Notes, Glossary, and Sources

NOTES

Knowing the references enhances the understanding of this material. It's helpful to know who the famous people are, and to understand the background of the places mentioned. Some notes on the translations are below, followed by a glossary of important words, and a brief description of major sources.

- All Chinese has been transliterated according to the pinyin system. The only exceptions are Tao (Dao), Confucius (Kong Fuzi), and dim-sum, because those terms are known by such long-standing spellings.
- In Chinese, the family name or "surname," comes first. For example, Bo Yi is from the Bo family.
- When the significance of a named person is no longer known, or where the names may have been arbitrary and fictitious, no explanation is given. Occasionally, a fictional name has an allegorical meaning, and in those cases, a literal translation is provided in parentheses. The birth and death dates of all real people have been provided at their first mention.
- It was common to refer to a person by more than one name, because most classical Chinese had several names at once—a child name, a personal name, an artistic name, an official name, a warrior name, a religious name, a posthumous name in some cases, and so on. Confucius, for example, is also known as Zhongni. Laozi is also known as Lao Dan. It's simply a part of literacy to know, and where relevant, alternative names are listed here.
- Dates before the common era (BCE) are noted as such. Otherwise, all dates are in the common era (CE).

Amitabha In Chinese, Mituo; the Buddha of the Western Paradise.

Bo Le A famous horse tamer and judge of horses from the Spring and Autumn period (c. 771–476 BCE). He was the retainer of Duke Mu of Qin (r. 659–621 BCE).

Bo Yi Along with his brother, Shu Qi, Bo Yi represents great moral virtue, loyalty, and pacifism in Chinese culture. Sometimes, the term, "Boyi" is taken to refer to both brothers. The two lived in the eleventh century BCE. At one point they openly opposed war by daring to pull on the emperor's chariot reins. They would have been killed on the spot had a general not recognized their virtue and saved them. But the war went forward, culminating in the violent Battle of Muye (c. 1046 BCE) The two brothers withdrew to a mountain and eventually died of starvation because they refused to eat the food of a government they now considered corrupt.

Bodhisattva A being who compassionately vows to liberate all sentient beings.

Buddha of Universally Pervading Superlative Wisdom In Chinese, Datong Zhisheng Fo, or in Sanskrit, Mahābhijñā-jñānābhibhū.

Chen (state) An ancient state located in present-day Henan Province. Established c. 1045 BCE and conquered in 479 BCE.

Chu (state) An ancient state in present-day Hubei and Hunan provinces. It was a viscounty before 704 BCE and a kingdom, 704–223 BCE.

Confucians Also known simply as the scholars, this term includes the philosophical followers of Confucius, as well as the literati that dominated imperial China.

Confucius A latinized form of Kong Fuzi, meaning "Master Kong" (551–479 BCE). His personal name was Kong Qiu. He was a teacher, editor, statesman, and philosopher. Confucius is traditionally credited with having authored or edited many of the Chinese classics, his thought shaped the whole of Chinese history for thousands of years, and his outlook is still a part of Chinese culture today. He was born in the district of Zou near the present-day city of Qufu, Shandong Province, taught seventy-two major disciples, and is buried in Qufu.

Dimsum The light refreshments or pastry, especially in Cantonese cooking. The proper romanization would be *dianxin*, with the word *dian* meaning dot or touch. In the story of Deshan (page 89), he asks the woman for dimsum, which could simultaneously imply "touches of heart." That's why she later asks him what heart he intends to touch in a play on the same words.

Duke Wen of Teng Monarch of the state of Teng in the Warring States Period (475–221 BCE), he ascended to the throne in 326 BCE.

Early Kings *Xianwang* refers generally to ideal early rulers. They represent leaders who were wise, cultured, altruistic, unselfish, and peaceful. At times, the term refers to the earliest legendary rulers; see the *Three Kings,* and the *Three Sovereigns and Five Emperors.*

Five Crops Millet, soybeans, sesame, barley, rice.

Five Grains There was an ancient belief that eating the Five Grains fed the Three Worms and that this resulted in an early death.

Five Phases One of the most important of Chinese metaphysical, philosophical, and medical theories, the Wu Xing or Five Phases address the fundamental energies of the world. Although the terms seem material, the words are symbols of five kinds of change: Wood (stiffening, rising upward), Fire (hot, bright, expanding, drying), Earth (leveling, neutralizing, harmonizing), Metal (congealing, consolidating, hardening), and Water (liquid, downward, flowing, cold, damp).

Five Stars Mercury, Venus, Mars, Jupiter, and Saturn.

He Xu A tribal chief of the Huaxia nationality in the Spring and Autumn Period (c. 771–476 BCE).

Heaven In Chinese, this is the word *tian,* which also means "sky." It is the eternal and supreme power in the world. Although it is regarded as having a will—in that its actions change human and natural life and cannot be resisted—it is not a personage. Neither is it the residence of a god or gods nor a place for an afterlife. Significantly, heaven is seen as the greatest initiating power, but it is not capable of doing everything on its own. That's why it is paired with earth, for what heaven initiates—weather, sun and moon, the seasons—earth must receive, nurture, and grow.

Huizi A philosopher representing the School of Names (sophists or dialecticians), named Hui Shi (370–310 BCE). While his own works are no longer extant, the *Zhuangzi* mentions him thirty-five times and he appears in conversation with Zhuangzi.

Immortals Known as *xian,* these are either legendary immortals or an honorific name for highly advanced Taoists.

Jie The last ruler of the Xia Dynasty (c. 2070–c. 1600 BC) was Jie of Xia (1728–1675 BCE). He is regarded as a tyrant, oppressor, and responsible for the downfall of the dynasty.

Jin'guancheng An alternate name for Chengdu, Sichuan Province.

Kalpas A Sanskrit word meaning an eon, or period of inconceivably long time as defined in Hindu and Buddhist cosmology.

Kui-demon The kui was a one-legged mountain demon in Chinese mythology.

Lao Dan Another name for Laozi.

Laozi "Lao" means old or venerable, so Laozi can be thought of as "a man who is old and venerable." His given name was Li Er (sixth–fifth centuries BCE) and he is also known as Lao Dan. He was an official in the imperial archives of the Zhou Dynasty (1046–256 BCE), and is the author of the *Daodejing*.

Lu A vassal state of the Zhou Dynasty that existed from c. 1042–249 BCE. It was famous as the home state of Confucius.

Mahakashyapa One of Buddha's principal disciples from the kingdom of Magadha (in ancient India).

Mohists These were the followers of the philosopher, Mozi (c. 468–c. 391 BCE). His original name was Mo Di, and his named is latinized as Micius. He was strongly opposed to both Confucianism and Taoism. He emphasized self-restraint, self-reflection, and authenticity, and he disdained the Confucian concept of the Rites. Mohism declined in the third century BCE, and mostly disappeared by the third century CE.

Mount Grdhrakuta One of several sites at which the Buddha and his monks spent the rainy seasons in India. The peak was said to resemble a vulture's head.

Mount Tai Taishan is the first of the Five Sacred Mountains of China and is located in Shandong Province.

Nirvana A transcendent state without suffering, desire, nor sense of self, with a person released from karma and the cycle of death and rebirth. It represents the goal of Buddhist liberation from the cycle of transmigration.

Noble one The Chinese term is *junzi*, and it originally meant a ruler or an aristocrat. It was expanded to also mean a cultivated person who tried to perfect themselves and who would then be an exemplar for self-cultivation in the world. Older translations use terms such as "gentleman" and "superior person."

Nonaction This is the famous term, *wuwei*. That literally means "not doing" or nonaction. It really means to live as naturally as possible and not to scheme for any covetous outcome.

Pei Now a county in Jiangsu Province.

Prajnaparamita The highest form of Buddhist perfected wisdom.

Prime Minister of Shu This poem is about Zhuge Liang (181–234), who was also known as Kong Ming. He was the prime minister of the state of Shu Han during the Three Kingdoms Period. Du Fu wrote the "Prime Minster of Shu" after visiting the Wuhou Shrine in Chengdu, Sichuan Province, which is dedicated to Zhuge.

Qi (state) A duchy (1046–323 BC) and then a kingdom (323–221 BCE), located in present-day Shandong Province.

Qin (musical instrument) Also called a *guqin* ("ancient zither"), the qin is a seven-stringed zither and it is the premier instrument for the scholar, recluse, sage, or cultivated person in classical Chinese society. It has no frets and is often played solo. The qin is considered to be the "father of all Chinese music," and the "instrument of the sages."

Qin (state) This ancient Chinese state (ninth century–221 BCE) in the north central area of present-day China, eventually unified all of China in 221 BCE for the first time.

Qin to Chu Qin and Chu were two neighboring states in ancient China.

Shakyamuni Buddha This historical Buddha, also known as Gautama Buddha (fourth–sixth centuries BCE). He was believed to have taught mostly in the eastern part of ancient India.

Shang The Shang Dynasty (c. 1600–1046 BCE) occupied an area of northeastern China centered around the Yellow River valley.

Shi'nan Yiliao Name of a character in the *Zhuangzi*.

Shun Emperor Shun, or Yu Shun (c. 2294–2184 BCE), was a legendary ruler, and one of the Three Sovereigns and Five Emperors. Shun was famous as a paragon of modesty, filial piety, humility, and enlightened rule.

Six Energies The Chinese term, "Liu Qi," comprises wind, cold, summer, wet, dry, and fire. When these primal energies are discordant, then the climate becomes abnormal.

Solution of Nine A unit of ninety. Ninety days multiplied over the four seasons would give a theoretical year of 360 days.

Son of Heaven The emperor.

Song (state) An ancient feudal state established in the eleventh century BCE and conquered by the state of Qi in 286 BCE. It was located in northeast China.

Song Yuan Jun Duke Yuan of Song (r. 531–517 BCE).

Three Kings They were: Xia Yu (Yu the Great; c. 2200–2100 BCE), Shang Tang (c. 1675–1646 BCE), King Wu of Zhou (r. 1046–1043 BCE). All three were considered good and wise rulers.

Three Sovereigns and Five Emperors The Three Sovereigns were Suiren, Fuxi, and Shenong. The Five Emperors were the Yellow Emperor and his sons, Zhuan Xu, Di Ku, Tang Yao, and Yu Shun.

True Person A name for an accomplished Taoist. The Chinese term is *zhenren*. Zhen means, "true, realized, genuine."

Wei (state) An ancient state (403–225 BCE) in parts of present-day Henan, Hebei, Shanxi, and Shandong Provinces.

Weiqi Known by its Japanese name, Go, this is a board game where two players aim to surround the most territory. It was invented in China more than 2,500 years ago and is considered to be the world's oldest board game. The playing pieces consist of identical round stones, one side being black and the other white, and they are placed on the intersections of a grid of nineteen × nineteen squares. The Chinese legend of its origin is that Emperor Yao (2337–2258 BC) ordered his counselor Shun (c. 2294–2184 BCE) to design the game to teach discipline and foresight to his son, who was both a vicious man and a playboy.

Xie Sanlang An eminent monk of the Tang Dynasty also known as Shi Bei.

Yan (state) An ancient Chinese state whose capital of Ji became Yanjing and eventually Beijing. It was established in the eleventh century BCE and was conquered in 221 BCE.

Yan Hui Sometimes known simply as Hui (521?–481 BC), he was the favorite disciple of Confucius.

Yao Emperor Yao, or Tang Yao (c. 2356–2255 BCE), was a legendary ruler, and one of the Three Sovereigns and Five Emperors. He is regarded as having been a morally perfect and intelligent sage-king.

Yellow Springs Deep underground springs and the mythological realm of the dead.

Yi Qiu Active during the Warring States period, Yi Qiu (475–221 BCE) was a grandmaster of weiqi.

Ying Probably a place in present-day Shandong Province.

Yu the Great A legendary ancient ruler, Yu the Great (c. 2200–2101 BCE) was known for engineering flood control, beginning dynastic rule in China by establishing the Xia Dynasty (c. 2070–c. 1600 BCE), and for having high moral character.

Zengzi A student of Confucius named Zeng Shen.

Zhongni Another name for Confucius.

Zhou Yin Zhou, Di Xin, or Zhou of Shang (1105–1046 BCE) was the last ruler of the Shang Dynasty (c. 1600–1046 BCE). He is regarded as one of the most vile and corrupt rulers in all Chinese history.

Zhou (state) This state was an early and the longest-lasting of Chinese dynasties (1046–256 BCE).

Zilu A student of Confucius also called Zhong Yu.

Zizhang A student of Confucius, also known as Zhuansun Shi.

SOURCES

Analects Known in Chinese as *Lunyu,* or *Edited Conversations,* this is a collection of sayings and ideas attributed to Confucius. The book was compiled by his followers in the Warring States era (475–221 BCE).

Art of War The *Sunzi Bingfa* is a military treatise that dates from the fifth century BCE. The book has remained one of the primary sources of strategy ever since, and it has influenced military studies, business tactics, and legal strategy.

Book of Rites Titled *Liji* in Chinese, this collection of texts describes the social forms, administrative standards, and ceremonial rites of the Zhou Dynasty (c. 1046–256 BCE). The book was first compiled in the Warring States era (475–221 BCE) and was revised several times.

Classic of Poetry Known in Chinese as *Shijing,* this oldest collection of poetry dates from the eleventh–seventh centuries BCE and contains 305 poems. It is said to have been edited by Confucius.

Daodejing This book is one of the primary texts of Taoism and has become a part of world philosophy. Its actual date and authorship is undecided, but the received tradition states that the book was written by Laozi in the sixth century BCE. It is also known as the *Tao Te Ching* (an earlier transliterated title) or referenced after its author's name as the *Laozi*. The name *Daodejing* literally translates to "Tao-Virtue-Classic," with the word "jing" or "classic" being the designation for a canonical work. The book of roughly 5,000 words, divided into eighty-one chapters, is a fundamental text for both philosophical and religious Taoism, and it influenced other schools, such as Legalism, Confucianism, and Chinese Buddhism (especially Chan or Zen Buddhism, which uses many Taoist words and concepts). Chinese poets, painters, calligraphers, and even garden designers have used the *Daodejing* for inspiration. Its influence has also spread widely outside of Asia and it is among the most translated books.

Mengzi This book was named after its author, Mengzi (372–289 BCE), whose named was latinized as Mencius. He is considered the second most prominent Confucian philosopher after Confucius. The *Mengzi* is a collection of anecdotes and records of conversations regarding moral and political philosophy between Mengzi and the rulers of several of the Warring States.

Wenzi A Taoist classic that was written by a disciple of Laozi, according to the received tradition. The earliest discovered version dates to a 55 BCE tomb. Little is reliably known about Wenzi, but his book's place in Taoist literature is unquestioned.

Wumenguan The translation of the very title is difficult. At the least, the book is named after its author, the Chan (Zen) master, Wumen Huikai (1183–1260). Wumen means "no-gate." The word *guan* in the title can mean "mountain pass; to close; to shut; to turn off; to concern; to involve." Translating it as the *Mountain Pass of No-Gate* seems to address most of the multiple meanings. The book is a compilation of forty-eight Chan cases, or *gong'an* (koan, in Japanese), deliberately paradoxical Buddhist lessons to spur students toward realization.

Xunzi Attributed to Xun Kuang, a third century BCE Confucian philosopher, addressed as Xunzi, or Master Xun, this text places a strong emphasis on learning and propriety.

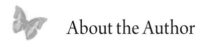 About the Author

Deng Ming-Dao is an author, artist, teacher, and book designer. He has been writing about Taoism and Chinese philosophy since the early 1980s and his books have been translated into eighteen languages. His primary Taoist teacher was Kwan Saihung, the subject of *The Chronicles of Tao*, but he has also studied with a number of other teachers as well.

His woodcut prints are in the collections of the Fine Arts Museum of San Francisco, Achenbach Foundation; Brooklyn Museum; Oakland Museum; Plains Art Museum; as well as corporate and private collections.

Deng Ming-Dao has trained in a variety of Chinese martial arts since 1975. He has been most involved with the internal systems of Xingyiquan, Baguazhang, and Taijiquan. He teaches periodically in seminars across the country.

Hampton Roads Publishing Company
... *for the evolving human spirit*

Hampton Roads Publishing Company publishes books
on a variety of subjects, including spirituality, health,
and other related topics.

For a copy of our latest trade catalog, call (978) 465-0504
or visit our distributor's website at *www.redwheelweiser.com*.
You can also sign up for our newsletter and special offers by going to
www.redwheelweiser.com/newsletter/.